Fake Meds Online

Alexandra Hall • Georgios A. Antonopoulos

Fake Meds Online

The Internet and the Transnational Market in Illicit
Pharmaceuticals

Alexandra Hall
School of Social Sciences
Business and Law
Teesside University
Middlesbrough, United Kingdom

Georgios A. Antonopoulos
School of Social Sciences
Business and Law
Teesside University
Middlesbrough, United Kingdom

ISBN 978-1-137-57087-1   ISBN 978-1-137-57088-8   (eBook)
DOI 10.1057/978-1-137-57088-8

Library of Congress Control Number: 2016953819

© The Editor(s) (if applicable) and The Author(s)2016
The author(s) has/have asserted their right(s) to be identified as the author(s) of this work in accordance with the Copyright, Designs and Patents Act 1988.
This work is subject to copyright. All rights are solely and exclusively licensed by the Publisher, whether the whole or part of the material is concerned, specifically the rights of translation, reprinting, reuse of illustrations, recitation, broadcasting, reproduction on microfilms or in any other physical way, and transmission or information storage and retrieval, electronic adaptation, computer software, or by similar or dissimilar methodology now known or hereafter developed.
The use of general descriptive names, registered names, trademarks, service marks, etc. in this publication does not imply, even in the absence of a specific statement, that such names are exempt from the relevant protective laws and regulations and therefore free for general use. The publisher, the authors and the editors are safe to assume that the advice and information in this book are believed to be true and accurate at the date of publication. Neither the publisher nor the authors or the editors give a warranty, express or implied, with respect to the material contained herein or for any errors or omissions that may have been made.

Cover illustration: Modern building window © saulgranda/Getty

Printed on acid-free paper

This Palgrave Macmillan imprint is published by Springer Nature
The registered company is Macmillan Publishers Ltd.
The registered company address is: The Campus, 4 Crinan Street, London, N1 9XW, United Kingdom

ACKNOWLEDGEMENTS

We both thank a number of individuals and organisations for providing us with valuable time and support while working on this project. Andrea Di Nicola, Elisa Martini and members of eCrime at the University of Trento for their collaboration over the last few years. Our colleagues and friends at Teesside University, especially Paul Crawshaw, Steve Hall, Mark Horsley, Joanna Large, Georgios Papanicolaou, Anqi Shen, Louise Wattis, Philip Whitehead and Simon Winlow. The participants who facilitated the study, many of whom cannot be named. Of those who can, sincere thanks to Danny Lee-Frost and Alistair Jeffrey from the Medicines and Healthcare products Regulatory Agency (MHRA) for the provision of data and investigative files. Finally, thanks to Jules Willan at Palgrave for being such a pleasure to work with.

Alexandra Hall thanks her co-author Georgios A. Antonopoulos for the opportunity to work on such an interesting project and for his encouragement and support during the early stages of her academic career. She also thanks Roop Sagar and Natasha Boojihawon at Union Street Media Arts (www.unionstreetmediaarts.co.uk) for their friendship over the years, and for their help in improving her graphic design skills. Most of all, she thanks her family: Michael, Mam, Dad, Christopher and Granda—thanks for your continuous love, support, personal and intellectual inspiration. I could not have done this without you.

Georgios A. Antonopoulos thanks Alexandra Hall for her incessant enthusiasm, her hard work and the wonderful collaboration. Moreover, he thanks Lorenza Antonucci, Rob MacDonald, Petrus van Duyne, Klaus von Lampe, Jackie Harvey, Almir Maljevic, Melvin Soudjin and Edward

Kleemans, as well as the participants of the 2014 Cross-Border Crime Colloquium in Sarajevo, for the interesting discussions on an aspect of the book that was presented there. He is also indebted to the Centre for Criminological Research at the University of Sheffield and Free University of Amsterdam for their hospitality in July and November 2015, respectively. Finally, he thanks Rena, Apostolis, and, of course, Sparky for the constant company during the writing of the book.

CONTENTS

1 Introduction   1

2 The Online Trade in Illicit Pharmaceuticals:
   The UK Context   19

3 The Demand Side   47

4 The Supply Side   79

5 Conclusion   113

Bibliography   119

Index   137

LIST OF ABBREVIATIONS

B2B	Business-to-business
B2C	Business-to-consumer
C2C	Consumer-to-consumer
DTCA	Direct-to-consumer advertising
EMA	European Medicines Agency
FDA	Food and Drug Administration
ICT	Information and communications technology
IOP	International Online Pharmacy
IPR	Intellectual property rights
ISP	Internet service provider
LEA	Law enforcement agency
MHRA	Medicines and Healthcare Products Regulatory Agency
NCA	National Crime Agency
OP	Online pharmacy
OTC	Over-the-counter
PIEDs	Performance and image-enhancing drugs
POM	Prescription-only medicine
R&D	Research & development
UK	United Kingdom
WHO	World Health Organisation

LIST OF FIGURES

Fig. 2.1   Table of counterfeit seizures   26
Fig. 2.2   Graph highlighting the distribution of web-hosting companies
           used by illegal online pharmacies   36
Fig. 2.3   Graph highlighting the percentage of online pharmacies with or
           without a physical address   37
Fig. 2.4   Affiliate brands promoted by spam, June 2010   38
Fig. 4.1   Map highlighting global flows of illicit medicines   91

CHAPTER 1

Introduction

Abstract This chapter outlines the book's rationale and analytical approach, one that embeds an original empirical dataset in an integrated theoretical framework. It introduces the reader to a number of complex and interdependent forces, processes and spaces that are analysed as co-constitutive in the chapters that follow. The chapter also outlines the methodology in detail, including a discussion of the ethics of online research. It finishes by summarising the main definitional issues surrounding the illicit medicine trade.

Keywords medicines • counterfeit • falsified • substandard • FAKECARE project

There is a burgeoning global trade in counterfeit, falsified, unlicensed and substandard medicinal products. Recent estimates claim that the trade has grown by 90 per cent since 2005, with an approximate turnover of $200 billion, suggesting it has now overtaken marijuana and prostitution as the largest illicit market for traffickers (IRACM 2013; see also Finlay 2011). This increase has been particularly apparent in the context of various evolutionary phases in information and communications technologies (ICTs) and electronic commerce since the late twentieth century (Kovacs Burns and Morrice 2004; Jopson 2013; see also Yingqun 2013; Keeling 2014; Lavorgna 2015), and the Internet now acts as the main avenue through which this criminal market is expanding. Yet, despite growing

© The Author(s) 2016
A. Hall, G.A. Antonopoulos, *Fake Meds Online*,
DOI 10.1057/978-1-137-57088-8_1

public concern and media attention (Boseley 2008; Clark 2008; Jack 2016), this extensive, extremely profitable and ultimately life-threatening[1] (see Fotiou et al. 2009; JDSU 2010; Mackenzie 2012; The New York Times 2012) online market has yet to be fully unpacked empirically or theoretically by criminologists and sociologists (for exceptions see Yar 2008; Lavorgna 2015).

This book attempts to fill that gap by offering the first in-depth and empirically grounded social scientific analysis of the *online trade in illicit medicinal products*. Using the UK as a case study—one of the largest and most lucrative European markets for pharmaceuticals (Morgan 2008) and a context in which R&D in pharmaceuticals has the largest investment in Europe (EFPIA 2012)—the main aim is to analyse the cultural, technological and politico-economic forces currently shaping this historically unique criminological phenomenon. Importantly, we offer an empirical and theoretical analysis of both the *supply* and *demand* dimensions of the trade in the UK. Therefore, the book lies at the intersection of research on illicit markets, cybercrime, intellectual property crime, medical sociology and digital culture. Discussions will include analyses of the relationships between technology and pharmaceutical counterfeiting, 'organised crime' and the global political economy, Web 2.0 and late-modern health practices, and the Internet, drugs and consumer culture (see Power 2013).

In order to offer a thorough exploration of the nature and dynamics of this complex and often paradoxical illicit market, it is necessary to expand the scope of our analysis of illicit medicines, their online trade and its social organisation. Epistemologically, our research offers an examination unconstrained by disciplinary boundaries but committed to emerging trans-disciplinary and post-disciplinary paradigms (see Sayer 1999; Jessop 2004; Hall and Winlow 2015). In doing so it embeds an original empirical dataset in an integrated theoretical framework that borrows from criminology, critical political economy, consumer culture, medical sociology and digital and new media studies. Consequently, a number of complex forces, processes and spaces, routinely considered as disconnected in studies of crime and deviance for many years, can now be clearly seen as co-constitutive.

Firstly, our research aims to transcend the limitations of narrow work on illicit markets by incorporating a dialectical understanding of the material and the cultural. From the significance of production and distribution systems to everyday changes in the consumption of pharmaceuticals, interacting *politico-economic* and *cultural* processes and structures at work in this context will be explored as the analysis is embedded in a broader critical discussion of late-capitalism, its cultural phenomena, technological idiosyncrasies and systems of trade and commerce.

Secondly, adding to the previous point, simply externalising the trade by placing this illicit market outside of legitimate political and economic structures and legal companies that have a foundational influence on its functioning also weakens analysis and preventative action. As it will become clear later, the online trade in illicit medicines is rooted in a number of *licit* trade processes and practices. Therefore, the blurred distinction between *legality* and *illegality* is another dual category of exploration (see van Duyne 2003, 2005; Nordstrom 2007; Antonopoulos and Papanicolaou 2014).

Thirdly, although the book's main aim is to unpack and analyse the *online* trade in illicit pharmaceuticals, its virtual elements cannot be divorced from the material goods being traded in the physical world. For instance, while ICTs enable further market reach in terms of their marketing and advertising functions, the trade is also systematically entrenched in such things as container-based shipping and the seaport trade. We must also emphasise the distinct corporeal nature of the products being exchanged. Ultimately this is a computer-aided crime, whereby digital technologies are in effect propagating a trade in material goods traditionally done offline (Wall 2007; Yar 2013). Therefore, the symbiotic relationships between *online* and *offline* spheres are analysed throughout.

Fourthly, although the book focuses primarily on the UK, simply analysing one national context is problematic. After all this trade functions on a global scale yet is marked in national and local 'zones', often moving spatially through stages in the supply chain. For that reason we aim to embed our analysis of the trade in its varied yet simultaneous spatial scales throughout the book, without overlooking the UK as the main focus, by highlighting both *global* and *local* sites on which the market has emerged and developed over time (Hobbs 1998; Nordstrom 2007).

The interdependency of these categories and levels of enquiry is the basis upon which the book's critical analysis progresses. As the argument unfolds, the analysis will focus on the rise of the Internet as one factor working in conjunction with the non-digital in a dynamic way, along with a variety of transnational social, cultural, political and economic processes, to enable the supply and demand of illicit medicines in the UK. Furthermore, the research, some of which stems from the European project 'www.fakecare.com' (see below), also engages with policy and practitioner communities working at local, national and international levels. Therefore, the book acts as a social scientific analysis as well as a set of practical guidelines for law enforcement agencies (LEAs), regulatory agencies and customers at risk of consuming illicit medicines bought online.

Following this introductory chapter outlining the book's aims, structure, methodology, and the definitional issues surrounding the illicit medicine trade, Chaps. 2, 3 and 4 act as the substantive chapters based on our empirical research, each answering a number of specific research questions. Chapter 2 contextualises the expanding online trade in illicit medicines in the UK, offering an overview of the size, nature and dynamics of the trade and the facilitating role played by the Internet. Chapter 3 focuses on the demand-side and investigates the cultural and technological factors contributing to the growing consumption of illicit medicines bought online. Chapter 4 is an exploration of the supply side and explores the political economy and social organisation of the trade with regard to the physical flows of illicit medicines. The book ends with a final chapter offering concluding remarks.

The Project 'www.fakecare.com'

The initial idea for this book was realised as part of a wider project across European Union member states: 'www.fakecare.com' (hereafter, Fakecare). Coordinated by the eCrime group at the University of Trento (specifically Andrea Di Nicola and Elisa Martini) and financed by the European Commission under the programme ISEC 2011, the overarching aim of Fakecare was to develop expertise against the online trade in fake medicines by producing and disseminating knowledge, counterstrategies and tools across the EU. The project adopted an interdisciplinary approach, drawing on research and expertise from a range of fields, including criminology, sociology, law, political science, information science, health and medicine. Furthermore, a number of innovative research methods were employed, including virtual ethnographies, the creation of honey-pot websites, web surveys, legal framework comparisons, script analyses of investigative and judicial case files, and web content analyses (Di Nicola et al. 2016).

The wider study is currently impacting on law enforcement and health regulatory policy and practice across Europe. Specifically, an ICT tool—FAST—which has been developed and is fed by findings from the wider study, is being used by LEAs in a number of EU countries. This tool uses an algorithm to identify illegal online pharmacies (OPs). Moreover, guidelines have been produced for both LEAs (Hall et al. 2015) and customers at risk of buying falsified medicines online (Di Nicola et al. 2015). Our role as project partners focused predominantly on a criminological investigation in the UK. Alongside additional research we have undertaken, this book specifically draws upon data collected via the UK-based virtual ethnography and the analysis of investigative and judicial case files collected as part of Fakecare, which we explain in more depth below. Therefore, data and findings from the UK report will appear in the book and any crossover is due to our involvement in the project (Di Nicola et al. 2016; see also Hall and Antonopoulos 2016a).

METHODOLOGY

This book is empirically grounded in over two years of fieldwork using a variety of research methods. The primary method was a virtual ethnography, which offered a nuanced way of researching the online trade in illicit medicines. We immersed ourselves in online communities and collected data from a range of sites deemed relevant to the research aims. The ethical issues of anonymity and confidentiality were of course considered—there is a fuller discussion of this issue below. Following a detailed discussion of the virtual ethnography, we will outline the additional methods and sources the book's findings rest upon, which include an offline ethnography, analyses of judicial and investigative case files, interviews with relevant stakeholders and enforcement officers, official statistics and secondary media and academic sources.

Virtual Ethnography

Traditionally, ethnographies were established as a means by which anthropologists and sociologists could explore cultural groups by using the technique of 'participant observation'. Observing and engaging with a specific group over an extended period of time allowed a 'thick description' (Geertz 1973), which contextualised human behaviour and everyday experiences, actions and practices. Ethnography and social research more generally has been compelled to account for the multi-sited, mobile and transnational nature of late-modern social, cultural, political and economic life. The traditionally local research sites of ethnographies have therefore been expanded to analyse global, 'glocal', transnational and virtual sites (see Wittel 2000). In the present-day context, everyday life for many includes a significant proportion of time spent in virtual communities. Whether in forums, blogs or social networking sites, social processes and patterns of communication take place in a new 'sphere' established by the Internet (Janetzko 2008: 161). This requires from the ethnographer a methodology able to offer insights into the virtual worlds we regularly inhabit. What is typically labelled 'virtual ethnography' or 'netnography' has steadily increased in usage to offer researchers greater insights into virtual communities (see, e.g. Ward 1999; Hine 2000; Fox et al. 2005b; Davey et al. 2012).

In short, traditional ethnographic methods—qualitative techniques used to interpret and detail in-depth a set of practices via an immersion in a given culture over time—are modified in order to interact in online communities and environments. Here, virtual ethnographic methods form the basis of our social scientific enquiry into the consumer demand and illicit supply of pharmaceuticals online in the UK. Considering the vast size of the global shadow economy, which the Internet, acting 'as a force multiplier' (Yar 2006: 10; Yar 2012, 2013), facilitates in all sorts of resourceful ways, online research must also try to better understand the aetiology—actors, causes and motivations—of cybercrime. Moreover, this research relates not only to criminal behaviour in terms of the suppliers of illicit medicines, but to the potentially deviant behaviour of online consumers either knowledgeably buying illicit medicines and/or purchasing prescription-only medicines (POMs) without prescription.

Primary data were collected via the virtual ethnography in both non-reactive and reactive ways (see Janetzko 2008). Initially, research began with a period of non-participant observation (sometimes referred to as 'lurking'), whereby observations were made across a range of online sites without direct interaction with users. This included taking screenshots of images and text from publicly available webpages including OPs, forums, social networking sites and classified advertising, as well as from a number of darknet sites, which were then coded and analysed. This was an invaluable primary stage of data collection that gave us the opportunity to familiarise ourselves with such a mass of information and specific interactions. We identified websites on the surface web claiming to be OPs via Google using the keywords 'online pharmacy UK' (42,000,000 results) and 'buy medicine no prescription UK' (59,200,000 results). The searches took place between June 2013 and March 2014. The OPs included were those offering POMs without prescription, delivered to UK addresses. Indeed, because test purchases were not made, the issue of whether these were fake websites set up to 'trap' buyers and defraud them or steal personal details is beyond the scope of this research. As we discuss below, we also gained access to data on illegal OPs via UK-based regulatory and LEAs. Furthermore, access to a number of relevant darknet sites was gained via an active criminal entrepreneur the first author interviewed as part of another research project (see Hall and Antonopoulos 2016b).

A period of reactive data collection online followed, where social media (Kaplan and Haenlein 2010) and forum profiles and email accounts were established in order to interact with users and take part in discussions with consumers and suppliers of medicines online. As previous research has shown, the use of social media platforms being used to access medical information has accelerated in parallel with the overall use of the Internet (Travers 2012). It would be impossible to research the entirety of the web or all active consumers in one nation state. Therefore, decisions were made to enter networks and online communities that appeared or claimed to cover UK contexts over certain periods of time. This was decided after general searches, observations and discussions with experts as to the most appropriate sites that individual users would use to discuss their experiences of buying and consuming specific prescription drugs and thus would be more likely to reveal information relating to where and who they purchased them from. Furthermore, we selected sites that were more likely to be targeted by illicit suppliers advertising and marketing their products online. Consequently, online forums and social networking sites constitute a large part of the sample of this virtual ethnography and were used as a means of both directly interacting with users and analysing already existing content. Just as Webber and Yip found in their analysis of the online trade in fake credit cards ('carding'), forums are a largely untapped resource of empirical criminological research data (Webber and Yip 2013: 193). A literature review and online searches via Google were used to identify and select forums that related to specific topics with links (unintended or otherwise) to pharmaceutical consumption, such as health, bodybuilding, sleep, weight loss, pro-anorexia, mental health, sexual health, men's and women's health, general forums with keyword searches, drug forums and their prescription drug sections, and pregnancy and motherhood.

On the demand-side, the virtual ethnography allowed an analysis of some of the online social networks that could potentially affect consumer decision-making about pharmaceuticals, consumers' buying habits, including the specific medicines being purchased, and the main determinant factors at play during purchases. With regards to the supply side, this method was used to observe and interact with illicit suppliers of medicines online. This included posing as customers in order to collect a number of specific details from a range of online sites. The data were then analysed, pooled and categorised in order to look for common patterns. The virtual ethnography allowed us to collect rich data from online sites used for supply and, when accompanied by data collected from other sources (see discussion below), to begin to analyse the networks that have proliferated throughout the various stages of the trade that caters for consumer demand in the UK.

Ethics

As a relatively new research methodology, various concerns regarding the ethical implications of virtual ethnographies have been raised, especially issues relating to anonymity, privacy and consent. In terms of consent, there is debate surrounding the 'public-ness' of Internet forums (see Lingel 2012; McKee 2013). On the one hand, a large amount of data collected online is in public online spaces where it must be assumed that users are aware that the information they post will be available to view. On the other hand, 'online interactions are sufficiently real for participants to feel they have been harmed or their privacy infringed by researchers' (Hine 2000: 23). Therefore, when data posted publicly are used for research purposes without informed consent, the researcher's intention is not to deliberately deceive or misinform the online participant. In most cases acquiring informed consent was attempted but unattainable due to the inconstant nature of the web. Moreover, although non-participant observation would be seen by some as unethical (see Fox et al. 2005b), this process was solely undertaken in publicly available sites and used as a way to review the online literature, learn the cultural language and get a feel for the space in order to establish the cultural knowledge and authority to interact in it and to later evaluate it; in other words to establish the research as a true ethnography (Thomsen 1998).

However, certain systematic practices were put in place to offer a certain amount of privacy to users. Following Davey et al.'s (2012) research into online drug forums, the practical ways in which this research endeavours to protect online populations are by concealing the usernames of contributors to the sites included in the research, and, where possible, abbreviating or re-wording large pieces of verbatim collected to prevent the identification of sources and users via online searches. Throughout the book, as a way of maintaining the ethical values of social research, data from the virtual environment (VE) do not appear alongside the user name, and forum and chat-room names are not disclosed. In a nutshell, the virtual ethnography is fully anonymised, and indeed 'double anonymised' in cases where forum users use pseudonyms.

Anonymity
The Internet offers counterfeiters opportunities to supply their products with a diminished 'paper trail', which reduces accountability and weakens enforcement, and provides consumers with convenient opportunities to buy medicines in relative anonymity. The subject of anonymity is, therefore, an important methodological issue to consider when researching online behaviour in this context. In a traditional ethnography the researcher can disguise an individual's or group's demographics at some point after adequate data have been gathered. However, the opportunity the Internet offers for user anonymity is one of the key determinant factors at play during the supply and purchase of particular medicines online; thus, it should not be seen as a problem in terms of the research, rather an interesting analytical issue to explore. The most obvious example is the online market in lifestyle drugs, such as those used to treat erectile dysfunction (ED). On these occasions, the anonymity the Internet offers consumers is fundamental to their decision to buy these products online (see Chap. 3; see also Koenraadt 2012). As Rodham and Gavin argue 'the anonymity of cyberspace allows Internet users to express themselves in ways that may be constrained in their real world interactions'. Drawing on recent research on identity, they note the enabling process the Internet offers for 'authentic' self-expression (2006: 95).

Yet this so-called authenticity has a criminological dimension because the Internet presents opportunities for the global trade in illicit medicines without the face-to-face interaction experienced by the patient and professional in traditional healthcare. Furthermore, consumer anonymity can be something of a misnomer. It functions in terms of offering a virtual supply of medicine for the consumer, which implies a certain amount of concealment, yet it is not genuinely anonymous; after all, the consumer's online details are often traceable and the products will be posted to their home address. Consequently, in this research, virtual practices are understood as everyday social practices with connections to real-world interaction and behaviour, and the *perceived* anonymity offered by the Internet is analysed as an important factor on the demand-side because it attracts consumer/patients online for pharmaceutical products—which can leave them at greater risk of consuming fakes and being exposed to their associated harms—and on the supply side because it offers the formation of cybercriminal relationships and a diminished paper trail.

To sum up so far, collecting data online, in this case studying the attitudes and practices of online consumers of pharmaceuticals, is a task which needs careful methodological and ethical consideration throughout the project (Hine 2000: 24). Online research requires a re-examination of traditional ethnographic methods, which, once adapted and combined with a solid analytical framework—one which in this case moves beyond the dichotomy of the 'real' and the 'virtual' to investigate online and offline interactions, and beyond the antagonisms that exist between economic, political and sociocultural analyses—can offer thick description and rich empirical data on the online cultural habits and behaviours of hard-to-reach and circumspect individuals and social groups. However, there are limits to using a virtual ethnography as an isolated method in this context. For instance, the researcher can only pool information that is available online. Moreover, this is a physical trade and, therefore, the distribution of the physical goods also requires investigation. For these reasons we also collected data from a range of other sources in order to triangulate the findings and offer richer empirical evidence.

Additional Methods

Data were also collected via traditional ethnographic methods. The primary research site for the offline ethnography was a gym in the Northeast of England. This involved immersing ourselves in a local gym culture, observing and interviewing illegal entrepreneurs involved in marketing and selling illicit medicines offline (some of whom had been supplied by online traders) and their customers who buy illicit medicines. In the context of the gym ethnography, we had the opportunity to acquire knowledge regarding the use of, and online trade in, illicit medicinal products with a primary focus on performance and image-enhancing drugs (PIEDs) including anabolic steroids (see Antonopoulos and Hall 2016). To a considerably lesser extent, data were also collected in relation to other PIEDs and pharmaceutical products. Furthermore, we conducted interviews and observations with a range of consumers and professionals outside of the gym setting, who predominantly reside in two urban areas in Northeast England and were accessed via our personal networks in these areas. As an addition to the purely textual analysis researchers are normally limited to a virtual ethnography, the offline interviews 'serve[d] as an effective means of triangulation and effectively improve[d] the credibility of the findings and the interpretations of the analysis' (Thomsen 1998). Interviews were conducted as free-flowing conversations with participants on a series of occasions between January 2014 and February 2015. Most of the interviews were quite informal and brief, in which a few questions were asked yet usable data were received and recorded as fieldwork notes (see Schwalbe and Wolkomir 2003).

Data from judicial and investigative cases, interviews with relevant stakeholders and enforcement officers, and secondary media and academic sources were also gathered and analysed. Specifically, we collected data where possible from the UK Medicines and Healthcare products Regulatory Agency (MHRA), National Crime Agency (NCA), INTERPOL and LegitScript. This included a number of semi-structured interviews and general discussions with experts in these organisations in the UK and Europe. We were able to gain first-hand knowledge from national and international regulatory and LEAs and investigators in the field who are already working to tackle the trade. For example, we interviewed analysts at INTERPOL's Medical Product Counterfeiting and Pharmaceutical Crime Sub-Directorate, a head analyst at the UK's National Cyber Crime Unit responsible for 'shutting down' illegal OPs, and the head of enforcement for the MHRA. Experts also provided us with some quantitative data. The NCA provided data regarding 1165 illegal OPs, which included information on domain names, registrars and registrants. The MHRA provided us with statistics relating to seizures of counterfeit medicines during raids from 2009 to 2014. We also gained access to a number of investigative and judicial case files relating to online pharmaceutical crime at the MHRA, which are presented in Chap. 4. The cases involve suppliers trading across the spectrum of illicit medicinal products, including instances of counterfeit, falsified and illegally supplied medicines (see discussion below). The majority include those specifically trading online, although one case relates to a large and well-known UK business whereby the products being traded were aimed at—and entered—the legitimate pharmaceutical supply chain. The details of this case are included because they offer a specific example of illegal parallel trade and an interesting insight into the actors and networks involved in the trade and routes through which illicit medicinal products enter the UK. Each case was initially summarised, before a script analysis scheme was written up.

Private stakeholders and commercial processes were also crucial aspects to investigate. We therefore interviewed and collected data from a leading pharmaceutical company and their in-house counterfeiting team and a large supplier of laboratory equipment, including data on supply chains and trafficking routes. The details of these companies will remain anonymous throughout the book. In addition, we attended the two-day workshop of the 'Pangea' single points of contact (SPoCs) at INTERPOL's headquarters in Lyon in March 2014, where representatives of LEAs (including INTERPOL, NCA, World Customs Organisation, etc.), health regulatory agencies (MHRA and FDA) and the private sector (MasterCard, Microsoft and LegitScript) were present to discuss various aspects of the 'Pangea' operation. This is an annual international operation that began in 2008, which is specifically aimed at tackling the online trade in illicit medicines by targeting the Internet service providers (ISPs), payments systems and delivery services implicated in the trade. 'Pangea' is coordinated by INTERPOL, the World Customs Organisation, Permanent Forum of International Pharmaceutical Crime (PFIPC), Heads of Medicines Agencies Working Group of Enforcement Officers (HMA WGEO), pharmaceutical industry and electronic payments industry. During the two-day workshop we obtained data from presentations and informal interviews with individuals from the aforementioned agencies and organisations, as well as from unpublished manuals and reports used by the authorities in various countries. Finally, secondary academic sources, media sources and open sources were reviewed and data from them were incorporated in the analysis. These included media, academic, jurisdictional and legislative reports, as well relevant research outputs from a number of European projects. All of the above methods were used, alongside our virtual ethnographic research, to build an accurate picture of the online trade in illicit medicines in the UK and are drawn upon in various ways throughout the book.

Limitations of Methods and Data

Our study presents some limitations, which should be acknowledged at this stage. Firstly, during ethnographic research there can be no guarantee that the information given is a wholly neutral representation of the activities and actors; one needs to remember that accounts offered in an ethnographic study are consciously or unconsciously interpreted by the researcher. Moreover, the data are limited to what the participants have provided and what the researcher has observed, and perhaps they cannot be generalised to the whole illicit medicine scene. In relation to the interviews with the informed actors there are issues of generalisability, and one can never be absolutely certain about validity, although 'member checking' significantly contributed towards eliminating untruthful accounts. In addition, there is also the issue of representativeness of the sample. In many instances researchers used a method of snowball sampling to identify participants, thus limiting the sample to the researcher's own personal network and their potential biases and, as a consequence, the scope of the findings (Levi 2015).

The second set of limitations is related to the accounts and data provided by the authorities. These are the result of law enforcement activity, which in turn is affected by resource restrictions, the competency of agents, organisational priorities and wider political priorities (see Hobbs and Antonopoulos 2014).

As one might expect, problems regarding validity and online research methods have also concerned some researchers, who argue that collecting trustworthy and representative empirical data online can be difficult. As Davey et al. (2012: 392) note 'forums are an unregulated, user-led source, information can be inaccurate or intentionally misleading'. Wittel (2000) acknowledges similar concerns:

> The first problem virtual ethnography has to face is the validity of data on the Internet users. The accuracy of information about age, gender, nationality etc. can hardly be checked. Instead of relying on hard facts, the ethnographer relies on the user's trustworthiness and on her own judgement. Moreover, this uncertainty is particularly problematic in a space that has become famous for its playful possibilities. To play with one's identity, to change one's real gender for a virtual one and by doing so to becoming someone else, someone whose chosen identity can be as real as the offline identity—all this is supposed to co-constitute the attraction of the Internet.

However, these problems can be overcome in some ways by 'checking the posters' credentials, evaluating the posts within a wider context and finding the same experiences or assertions reiterated elsewhere' (Rodham and Gavin 2006: 94). Moreover, many users are knowledgeable and informed, and play influential roles in disseminating information via forums to other users. Although some information may be inaccurate and some posts may be misleading, this should not lead to a general dismissal of data collected online. Data collected from online web forums and social networking sites can produce rich empirical evidence from normally hard-to-reach groups (in this case consumers and suppliers of illicit medicines online) and can offer tangible insights into the everyday life—values, attitudes and behaviours—of individuals and social groups in late-modern society. Indeed, collecting data offline does not consistently produce valid findings; face-to-face interactions can act to suppress true feelings that in some cases are more likely to be revealed in the anonymous online environment. In both instances the researcher is relying on the honesty and integrity of the participant (see Rodham and Gavin 2006: 94).

The final set of limitations is related to open sources. Not only do they most often refer to cases which the authorities came across, thus not reporting 'successful' criminal schemes, but they also tend to present the issues relating to the actors or the activity/market itself in a sensational and morally charged manner. In addition, material drawn from search engines depend on the researchers providing keywords, a process which may lead to the exclusion of reports that are peripherally relevant but extremely important for the wider context of the study (Jewkes 2011). Nevertheless, we think that the methodological triangulation throughout the study—involving both official and 'unofficial' sources—has created a net that has captured the most important aspects of the topic under investigation and we are confident that there is a high degree of validity in the findings.

A Composite Definition of 'Illicit Medicines'

Before we move onto our substantive chapters, it is important to point out the on-going debate surrounding the terminology used to define various categories of illicit medicinal product. Part of that debate relates to the separation of counterfeits from the market in falsified, substandard and unlicensed generic pharmaceutical drugs. The terminological debate has arisen because illicit medicine supply is not confined to trademark infringement alone, making any estimate that relies purely on counterfeit drug sales limited and the dark side of this crime type even more substantial. Furthermore, the regulatory and legal administration of medicines differs according to the type of illicit medicine being supplied, where it is produced, and where it is distributed and consumed. Adding to the confusion, various categories of both counterfeit and falsified medicines can be supplied by the same criminal actors and organisations. For example, our research found criminal organisations involved in selling a wide variety of illicit medicines simultaneously, often via a number of online sites.

As a result various terms are used to define categories of illicit medicines in different contexts. This includes *counterfeit medicines*, which are most often seen as those products infringing patents and intellectual property rights (IPR). According to the World Health Organisation (WHO):

> A counterfeit medicine is one which is deliberately and fraudulently misla-belled with respect to identity and/or source. Counterfeiting can apply to both branded and generic products and counterfeit products may include products with the correct ingredients or with the wrong ingredients, without active ingredients, with insufficient active ingredients or with fake packaging (WHO 2012, n.p.).

Although there is not enough space in this book to offer a critical exploration of IPR in this context (see Yar 2008: 65 for a short summary of the Agreement on Trade-Related Aspects of Intellectual Property Rights (TRIPS) in relation to counterfeit medicines), or of the political and economic interests of big pharma and their impact on the legitimate and illegitimate global pharmaceutical market (see Braithwaite 1984), there will be some discussion of the market in counterfeit medicines and its long and complex history and contemporary reality (see also Bate 2008).

Whereas counterfeits are those infringing IPR, *falsified medicines* are any fakes passed off by sellers as authentic medicines. The term falsification, therefore, moves beyond merely legal-economic terms relating to copyright infringement and embeds public health and the 'sticky subject' of generics in the definition (see IRACM 2013: 14). It is in this context that the European Commission now prefers to distinguish between falsified products and other categories of illicit medicine, including counterfeit medicines infringing IPR, as highlighted by the implementation of Article 1 of the Directive 2011/62/EU. According to the directive a falsified medicinal product is:

> [A]ny medicinal product with a false representation of: (a) its identity, including its packaging and labelling, its name or its composition as regards any of the ingredients including excipients and the strength of those ingredients; (b) its source, including its manufacturer, its country of manufacturing, its country of origin or its marketing authorisation holder; or (c) its

history, including the records and documents relating to the distribution channels used.[2]

Other illicit medicinal products include *unlicensed medicinal products*, otherwise referred to as *grey market products*. As we discuss in Chap. 2, variations in IP rights and licensing laws, where patent and trademark infringement in one country may differ in another, weakens regulatory standards and detection methods. Occasionally, traders dealing in generics or various branded products produced abroad yet sold in the UK seek to bypass existing IP laws and patents; these products may have been legally produced but are illegally supplied. Fakes in this instance include unlicensed products, which are those claiming to contain the identical active ingredients found in a formerly branded/patented product, or a product without a patent in the producing country, supplied via an unauthorised distribution channel in order to bypass existing IP laws and patents in the destination country. Furthermore, in the UK, legitimate generics are licensed and therefore authorised as copies of a formerly patented and branded drug. However, when a patent expires—one recent example in the UK being Viagra (sildenafil citrate) in 2013—an opening in the market for genuine and fake generics is created (see Chan 2013). One specific example is that of Kamagra, a sildenafil citrate-based ED drug legally produced in India, which is not licensed in the UK. According to the MHRA it is one of the most popular illicit medicines on the market; something our online research corroborates. We found a variety of online sites offering this product for sale as 'Generic Viagra' to UK customers. Finally, another category of illicit medicinal product is that of *substandard medicines* which, although genuine medicines produced by authorised manufacturers, do not meet the national quality standards set by the country in which they are being supplied.

Thus, both branded and generic pharmaceutical drugs can be falsified and both POMs and over-the-counter medicines (OTCs) can be falsified. Furthermore, this trade is not solely online: there is also a growing market of legally produced yet illegally supplied medicines entering the legitimate pharmaceutical supply chain (Yar 2012), the most prominent UK case of which is discussed in Chap. 4. In order to begin to overcome the definitional issues, policymakers have begun to focus their attention on the broader category of pharmaceutical crime and falsification rather than counterfeit medicines alone. On the one hand, as mentioned, the European Commission now prefers the term *falsified medicinal products*.

On the other hand, the WHO prefers the all-encompassing term *SFFC* (spurious/falsely-labelled/falsified/counterfeit) medicines. Overall, it is clear that reducing the illicit trade in medicines down to counterfeit products alone neglects the trade in substandard and unlicensed drugs. Throughout the book we will adopt the broad term *illicit medicines*, which includes falsified, substandard, unlicensed, illegally traded and counterfeit pharmaceuticals, while using more specific terms where necessary.

NOTES

1. One in four General Practitioners (GPs) in Britain report having treated people who bought medicines online for adverse drug reactions.
2. The Falsified Medicines Directive (Directive 2011/62/EU) was put forward by the European Commission in December 2008, published in July 2011 and applied on 2 January 2013. The directive can be accessed at: http://ec.europa.eu/health/files/eudralex/vol-1/dir_2011_62/dir_2011_62_en.pdf.

CHAPTER 2

The Online Trade in Illicit Pharmaceuticals: The UK Context

Abstract This chapter examines the online trade in illicit medicines in the UK, offering thick description and setting the background for the rest of the book. It begins by exploring the history of pharmaceutical falsification and how digital technologies increasingly facilitate the trade in illicit medicines. Next, it offers an overview of the size, nature and dynamics of the trade in the UK. This includes a discussion of the most popular illicit medicines being bought and sold online, and of the regulatory and legal framework currently in place to combat the trade. It finishes by examining the Internet infrastructure required to trade in illicit medicines online while avoiding detection, which include a number of tools, services and tactics.

Keywords illicit pharmaceuticals • cybercrime • internet infrastructure • online pharmacies

This chapter contextualises the online trade in illicit medicines, setting the background for the rest of the book. It begins by briefly historicising the interconnections between pharmaceutical falsification and digital technologies. Following this, the chapter discusses the nature and dynamics of the trade in the UK, which includes a short exploration of the most popular illicit medicines being bought and sold online, and of the legal

© The Author(s) 2016
A. Hall, G.A. Antonopoulos, *Fake Meds Online*,
DOI 10.1057/978-1-137-57088-8_2

and regulatory framework in place to combat the trade. The chapter finishes by summarising the Internet infrastructure required to trade in illicit medicines online, which includes outlining a typology of online sites, platforms and services used, the online marketing techniques employed, and the detection-avoidance tactics adopted by cyber-criminal entrepreneurs involved in the trade. The chapter attempts to provide preliminary answers to the following research questions:

- What is the relationship between pharmaceutical falsification and cybercrime?
- How has the online trade in illicit medicines developed over time?
- What is the distinct nature and dynamics of the UK market and which are the most popular illicit products being supplied?
- How effective is the legal and regulatory framework in place to combat the trade?
- What type of online infrastructure is required, and what are the main platforms and services used to advertise, market and sell illicit medicines online, while avoiding detection?

CYBERCRIME AND PHARMACEUTICAL FALSIFICATION: A VERY BRIEF HISTORY

Legal protection from counterfeiting in the form of Intellectual Property Rights (IPR) came into existence in Europe in the 1400s (Kangaspunta and Musumeci 2014). However, counterfeiting in the general sense of imitating and reproducing the work or creation of someone else without their authorisation has a much longer history. According to Rutter and Bryce instances of counterfeiting date back to 27 BC, appearing 'to have been used to generate profit and avoid taxation for almost as long as market and currency systems have existed to manage economic transactions' (Rutter and Bryce 2008: 1147). According to Bate, as intensive R&D products, counterfeit medicines have threatened our healthcare since the nineteenth century '[a]s technological capabilities advanced ... [and] counterfeiters turned to faking whatever goods were most profitable or most easily procured and distributed without detection' (Bate 2008: 2). By the late nineteenth century there were deep concerns in Britain about the adulteration of medicines which led to the passing of the Food, Drink and Drugs Acts of 1872 and 1875 and the Poisons and Pharmacy Act of 1908, as well as the publication of a series of 11 articles by Hopkins Adams in the US entitled 'The Great American Fraud' in which false claims about patent medicines were exposed (Dobson 2013). One well-known example of pharmaceutical 'tampering' occurred in 1982 when Johnson & Johnson found out that bottles of its extra-strength Tylenol capsules were laced with cyanide (JDSU 2010).

Since the late twentieth century, the international trade in both legitimate and illegitimate economies has expanded at an unprecedented rate, the result of which is that a vast amount of illicit goods—including counterfeits—now permeate the global market. The trade in counterfeit goods is estimated to account for anything up to seven per cent of world trade, equivalent to $500 billion (see Yar 2005), although more recent figures suggest an exponential growth over the last ten years, some suggesting counterfeiting and piracy cost the global economy $1.77 trillion in 2015 (World Economic Forum 2015: 3; see also UNODC 2015). This has been particularly apparent since the late 1970s, when specific political and economic events precipitated an ideological shift towards a neoliberal paradigm of competitiveness and openness in the global market economy (see Harvey 2005). Wholesale deregulation, the opening up of national economies to processes of globalisation and marketisation, and the proliferation of Special Economic Zones freed up the movement of capital and accelerated the financialisation of the global economy. These processes had concrete effects on criminality and a facilitating impact on the supply and demand of counterfeit goods; just as legitimate private industries profited from it, so too did the illegitimate industries that ran alongside them.

These macroeconomic processes had a formative effect on the growth of the illicit medicine market. According to official figures from the World Health Organization, by 2010 global counterfeit drug sales alone reached $75 billion. A 'conservative estimate' is that ten per cent of total pharmaceutical drug sales are counterfeit (Wertheimer and Wang 2012: 5; see also WHO 2012). Further statistics estimate that across the world up to one million people die each year after consuming counterfeit medicinal drugs (Southwick 2013), most of whom reside in developing nations. In Europe, according to a relatively recent study with 5000 European citizens across five nation states, five per cent of consumers suspected that they had received a counterfeit prescription drug while one per cent were sure they had. This suggests that up to 12.8 million consumers were exposed to counterfeit medicines in those countries (Jackson et al. 2012). Bearing in mind the broader focus here on illicit medicines, not counterfeits alone, and of the inherent dark nature of this illicit market, we can suspect that a much larger market is in operation, the true size and scope of which is currently opaque to statistical representations.

As we discuss further in Chap. 4, the differential characteristics of producer and consumer economies in a current global economy administered by deregulatory neoliberal politics foster the transnational trade in illicit pharmaceuticals. The traditional technique of *profit on alienation*—buying cheap in economically developing regions and selling dear in developed regions—has now been accelerated to an unprecedented speed and reach. Of particular importance is the active economic nexus that connects the socioeconomic advantages and consumer demands of industrialised nations to the cheap and often unregulated production centres in the manufacturing hubs of the world, predominantly in the emerging industrial economies of India and China. These hubs have a well-known history of pharmaceutical counterfeiting. In 2001, for example, Chinese authorities closed down 1300 illegal pharmaceutical factories after investigating 480,000 cases of counterfeit medicine production and distribution (Morris and Stevens 2006). In 2010, the Chinese State Food and Drug Administration revealed that by the middle of the year, the government had handed down penalties for 33,039 illegal online medicines advertisements and 1731 illegal medical device advertisements (CPB Review 2010). Moreover, the porous borders and global trade routes through which these products are imported, the development of outsourcing (Ryan and Sancilio 2013), the introduction of parallel trading practices and the differing effectiveness of legal frameworks addressing the issue across nation states present expanded opportunities for exploitation or circumvention by those involved in the trade (Vagg and Harris 2000; Hetzer 2002). Indeed, the attractions of this illegal market are obvious:

> [T]he demand for pharmaceutical drugs runs into hundreds of billions of dollars globally, and the returns on low cost production can be vast. For example, it costs $60/kg to buy a Viagra compound in China or India, which, when packaged in 25 mg tablets would sell on prescription in the US for up to $200,000. (World Finance 2012)

The ascendance of the neoliberal market economy was accompanied by advances in technology, communication and transport, adding further to the increased mobility of both physical and liquid capital across the globe. The 'borderlessness' of contemporary flows in consumer goods—which in practice increases movement in some respects while creating new borders in others—was made possible by new technologies such as container-based cargo shipping and aeromobility, advanced logistics, improved refrigeration, high-grade telecommunications and electronic money transfer systems (Sassen 1998; Urry 2013). Consequently, there is much debate questioning whether such technological innovations are changing the nature of modern criminality. Cybercrime is now an established research area in criminology, investigating the opportunities for crime and deviance offered or supported by new technologies and electronic communications (see Yar 2006; Wall 2007; Jewkes and Yar 2010). Accordingly, the relationship between cybercrime and the trade in counterfeit products and ideas is beginning to be better documented (Yar 2005, 2008; Wall and Large 2010; Treadwell 2011).

Technological capabilities allow for further counterfeiting because not only can better fakes be produced at a lower cost, but improvements in Information and Communication Technologies (ICTs) connects dispersed locations in global trade relations, making the formation of networks of buyers and sellers and the exchange of money relatively easy. This has become particularly apparent since use of the Internet and e-commerce by producers and consumers became widespread. During our initial exploration of the online trade in illicit medicines we found that the Internet plays a range of roles. Electronic transfer of money, online banking and shopping, the ease and affordability of building a website, the expansion of user-generated content and the sheer number of people now online are all factors that have expanded and proliferated a number of business-to-business (B2B), business-to-consumer (B2C) and consumer-to-consumer (C2C) marketplaces with huge market reach. These markets have been supplying all kinds of drugs—both legitimately and illegitimately—since the Internet's inception in the 1990s (see Walsh 2011). Our research found many online suppliers who can now offer a vast range of traditional and new synthetic psychoactive substances, performance-enhancing and pharmaceutical drugs. Other suppliers can offer active pharmaceutical ingredients (APIs) and the laboratory equipment needed to press and package pills (see Hall and Antonopoulos 2015; Antonopoulos and Hall 2016). Hence, the Internet has both simplified and accelerated the process of marketing and selling medicines and offered opportunities for those involved in the fake drug trade to widen their scope and customer base. In this respect the Internet acts as a time/space compressor, on the one hand connecting sellers with large numbers of consumers in dispersed locations and on the other offering the formation of transient relationships between (cyber)criminal entrepreneurs. As Guarnieri and Przyswa argue, the Internet is a mechanism allowing 'commercial connections of varying durability between individuals all responding to a common interest in making money' (2013: 221). Moreover, technological advances have also greatly increased the quality of imitation packaging so much so that it is largely impossible to distinguish an imitation from a genuine branded product (Wertheimer and Wang 2012: 4).

The expansion of the online trade in illicit medicines has occurred in parallel with developments in legal markets in pharmaceutical products. For instance, a significant development has taken place in Switzerland, the Netherlands and the UK, where the formation of companies such as www.aporose.ch, www.0800docmorris.com and www.pharmacy2u.co.uk has sought to supply not only their respective national markets but also neighbouring markets, exploiting the willingness of national health insurance funds to use online pharmacies as a way of lowering prescription expenditures (see Mossialos et al. 2004). The legitimate global online pharmacy market was estimated at US$ 15–20 billion in 2004 (see Laing and Mackey 2009), representing 15 per cent of the size of the legitimate industry (Bird 2008).

Significantly, e-commerce and the Internet's role in expediting the logical demands of the late-capitalist global market have encouraged a shift in import–export relationships and financial transactions. The specific digital infrastructure required to trade in illicit medicines online is discussed below, and throughout the book we will map out in more detail how the demand-side and supply side are embedded in specific political, economic, cultural and technological processes. Needless to say the trade is a growing global phenomenon with an extensive history.

THE ONLINE TRADE IN ILLICIT MEDICINES IN THE UK: A TRANSIT ZONE AND END-USER MARKET

In the UK it has been estimated that only one per cent of the medicines supplied are *counterfeit*, yet such is the size of the market that this equates 'to more than eight million packs of medicines worth about £425 million a year' (Clark 2008). It is widely argued, however, that the trade is growing and is significantly underestimated. For example, broader estimates of *falsified* products reveal that they make up as much as 50 per cent of the medicines bought online by UK consumers (Walsh 2011). Others have suggested that 16 per cent of UK consumers *knowingly* buy illicit medicines (Smithers 2013). However, in consideration of the problems associated with definitional issues and statistical estimates of the trade in illicit medicines, this section draws on our primary and secondary sources to offer a broad overview of the distinct nature of the online supply of illicit medicines in the UK, and to explore what role the UK plays in this transnational trade.

The UK is targeted by counterfeiters and those illegally trading in medicines for two main reasons: (1) it is a transit zone located between Asian producers and consumers in the USA and Western European countries, and (2) it is an end-user market targeted for higher profit margins due to the greater price of medicines and heightened consumption patterns in comparison to most other European countries. As a 'transit-point and end-user market' (Jackson et al. 2012), products enter the UK through less regulated and/or easily corrupted borders. As we discuss in Chap. 4, apart from a few small-scale operations illicit medicines are not produced in the UK and most are imported through a variety of trade routes. In a 2006 poll by the Pharmaceutical Security Institute highlighting the top ten countries where counterfeit drugs had been seized or discovered the UK was ranked seventh, with Russia and China first and second (PSI 2006), respectively. Interestingly, countries on the South Asian subcontinent were not included in the list, although it is widely believed that, along with Russia and China, a large proportion of illicit medicines entering the UK are produced in India and Pakistan. However, an interview with law enforcement in the UK revealed that this is the result of various international restrictions and less strict licensing opening up legal loopholes in South Asia. Moreover, there is an obvious dark side: some countries simply happen to have the most *reported* incidents of illicit medicines, whereas other countries lack the political will or resources to tackle the problem and thus do not produce statistics.

In a relatively recent 'crackdown' in the UK, in which when the Medicines and Healthcare products Regulatory Agency (MHRA), assisted by the police and the Home Office UK Border Force, raided addresses connected to the online supply of illicit medicines, a record amount was seized. The products found included '3.7 million doses of unlicensed medicines worth approximately £12.2 million, including 97,500 doses of counterfeit pills being seized in the UK worth £525,000' (MHRA 2013, n.p.). They included medicines used for hair loss, weight loss and erectile dysfunction (ED; MHRA 2013). Data we collected directly from the MHRA on counterfeit seizures during raids also identified the main medicines being supplied illegally as ED drugs (90 %), weight loss and hair loss medicines, which together were worth the amount in GBP over the last five years as shown in Fig. 2.1.

The 2010/2011 figure of £3,036,969 was characterised by two very large and related cases where shipments were seized en route to other markets. A head of enforcement at the MHRA substantiated the significant role that the UK plays as a transit point for illicit medicines, where shipments and postal packages that successfully reach the UK and receive a UK postal stamp can be rerouted with a heightened degree of 'legitimacy' attached. Another example of a seizure of illicit medicines transiting through the UK included a large shipment of counterfeit cancer drugs worth £200,000 intercepted in 2011/2012. They were not aimed at the UK market but on their way from Turkey via the EU (the UK) and destined for the USA. However, the MHRA representative also suggested that the nature of the supply chain is changing due to the greater risks associated with large shipments: 'We are now seeing much smaller parcels coming through the post from overseas, we expect this is in response to large parcels not wanting to be risked anymore.' Therefore, greater numbers of small-scale postal packages are beginning to shape the supply chain of illicit medicines targeting the UK market, the sheer size of which has a negative impact on seizure results. We were informed by law enforcement and customs officers that the majority of illicit medicinal products remain undetected as the sheer volume leaves institutional actors unable to prevent them from entering the country, a problem that once again reminds us of the limitations associated with official statistics.

Year	Amount in £
2009 /10	£598,770
2010 /11	£3,036,969
2011/12	£538,000
2012/13	£98,692
2013/14	None

Fig. 2.1   Table of counterfeit seizures (*Source*: UK Medicines and Healthcare Products Regulatory Agency (MHRA) 2014)

The Most Popular Illicit Medicines in the UK

The popularity of various medicines being supplied illegitimately around the world depends on the profile of the target market. The main factors that determine differences in demand are nation, culture and type of healthcare system. Developing nations are targeted by criminals selling counterfeit, falsified and substandard medicines at a cheaper price in bulk, profiting from volume and benefiting from lower regulatory standards. The size of the market and lack of regulatory bodies and affordable health-care renders this population at high risk of consuming illicit medicines. The largest consumers of illicit *lifesaving* medicines are, therefore, rural areas in developing nations, particularly parts of sub-Saharan Africa. In these regions key targets for the suppliers are 'high volume' drugs used to treat 'HIV, malaria, tuberculosis, hypertension, acid reflux, diabetes and hyperlipidaemia' (Wertheimer and Wang 2012: 6). Often the illicit medicine trade is the only source of pharmaceutical products in these areas. Furthermore, large amounts of substandard medicines are traded to developing nations by *legal* companies. During an 'off the record' con-versation with an employee of a major western pharmaceutical company, it was suggested that the legitimate pharmaceutical industry target spe-cific end-user markets depending on the quality of the products and the regulatory frameworks in place in different jurisdictions, with Africa a 'hot bed' and Japan a 'no go area' for trade in substandard products. Similarly, Nordstrom's (2007) research found legally produced substandard phar-maceuticals 'dumped on unsuspecting populations' in Africa, calling into question the assumption that 'street vendors and counterfeit factories are responsible for the majority of substandard drugs' (2007: 133).

Alongside the aforementioned role played as transit points, one of the primary supply drivers moving illicit medicines into developed states such as countries in Western Europe, the USA and Australia is the lucrative nature of the markets where higher profit margins make activities worthwhile. As Wertheimer and Wang (2012) note, in developed countries the target drugs for counterfeiters 'are newer ones with active patents that tend to be expen-sive. Examples are lifestyle drugs such as Viagra, psychiatric drugs, cancer drugs, steroids, hormones and monoclonal antibodies' (Wertheimer and Wang 2012: 6). In the highly individualised culture and privatised economy of the USA and Australia, there is an online demand for most Prescription Only Medicines (POMs) and Over the Counters (OCTs). However, in the UK, where an individualised culture exists in tension with a collectivised and subsidised healthcare system, we find that the demand in *lifesaving* medicines drops while demand in *lifestyle* drugs increases. Lifestyle drugs are medicines consumed according to personal choice and often for cosmetic reasons including the reversal of hair loss or the acceleration of weight loss, or for personal problems such as sexual dysfunction, all of which are indicated by the seizure results in the UK (MHRA 2013). Rarer medicines include opioids, sedatives, antibiotics and stimulants. Likewise, research undertaken by the Royal Pharmaceutical Society reported that two million UK consumers buy their medicines online and the most popular brands are Valium, Viagra and Prozac (BBC Online 2008).

Research undertaken as part of Fakecare found that in most European states there is a larger illicit market in lifestyle medicines. There is also, however, a growing market in falsified lifesaving medicines used to treat serious illnesses including cancer and HIV (Di Nicola et al. 2016). Specifically, our research in the UK found that the principal categories of medicine being falsified and sold via illicit suppliers are medicines to treat ED, anabolic steroids (both injectable and tablets), weight loss drugs/appetite suppressants, hair loss medicines, sedatives (including a large market in benzodiazepines and non-benzodiazepines), opioid analgesics, antibiotics, psychiatric drugs (including anti-psychotics and anti-depressants), fertility drugs, stimulants and, in rarer cases, medicines to treat cancer, HIV, diabetes, arthritis and hepatitis. Indeed, the research found that most POMs are available via sites that are likely to be supplying fakes, but that the largest consumer demand via illegitimate sites is for ED medicines, anabolic steroids and other lifestyle drugs, as well as a sizeable demand for sedatives, opioids and stimulants. This pattern relating to the types of medicines being supplied was supported by our UK-based online and offline ethnographies, statistics from the MHRA (see above), statistics gathered from the in-house counterfeiting team of a large pharmaceutical company and interviews with regulatory agencies and pharmaceutical companies. The factors contributing to the consumer demand for these products in the UK are explored in more depth in Chap. 3.

The Legal and Regulatory Framework

Bearing in mind the aforementioned difficulties associated with categorising illicit medicines, the legal and regulatory frameworks in place to combat medicine imitation are just as convoluted. Across the globe, there are variations in national regulatory frameworks and law enforcement priorities, and differing proportions of resources are spent on the pharmaceutical trade and its criminal equivalent. For instance, lax licensing laws in India contrast sharply with tight regulation in European states, which is one operative reason why India has become the world's leading producer of counterfeit and generic drugs (see Wertheimer and Wang 2012: 6; Chap. 4). Regulating such global disparity at the points of production and distribution is extremely difficult, but the Pangea operation is a relatively recent international development that seeks to bring together expertise from across national and institutional boundaries to tackle the trade. This is an annual international operation that began in 2008 and takes place for one week of each year. It is specifically aimed at tackling the online trade in counterfeit and illegal medicines. Pangea is coordinated by INTERPOL, the World Customs Organisation, the Permanent Forum of International Pharmaceutical Crime (PFIPC), the Heads of Medicines Agencies Working Group of Enforcement Officers, the pharmaceutical industry and the electronic payments industry.

The UK has a relatively strong regulatory framework. Pharmaceutical products must undergo a process of licensing via the MHRA or European Medicines Agency before they can be authorised for distribution. The MHRA is also the main body in the UK responsible for legal enforcement relating to the illicit medicine trade. However, the regulatory and legal administration also differs according to the type of illicit medicine being supplied. In the legal enforcement process in the UK the ability to prosecute offenders involved in the supply of illicit medicines varies according to whether they are selling either counterfeit or falsified medicines. There are four main avenues of prosecution the MHRA can use in order to pursue offenders. Firstly, they rely primarily on offences contained within the Medicines Act 1968, which carries a two-year maximum sentence and/ or unlimited fine. Secondly, the Trade Mark Act of 1994 for those cases where the product is deemed counterfeit carries a maximum of ten years. Thirdly, the Proceeds of Crime Act 2002 carries a 14-year maximum sentence. Fourthly, the most recent tool being used by UK authorities to prosecute offenders involved in the trade is the Fraud Act 2006, which carries a ten-year maximum sentence. However, the legal enforcement for sales of illicit steroids (as both pharmaceuticals under the Medicines Act 1968 and as a Class C drug under the Misuse of Drugs Act 1971) in the UK is currently under the remit of the police, not the MHRA (see

Antonopoulos and Hall 2016). For consumers, possession of illicit pharmaceuticals is not criminalised unless the medicine is controlled under the Misuse of Drugs Act 1971, which includes such medicines as oxycodone bought without prescription.

However, although the current regulatory administration in the UK involves a number of agencies that work to regulate the industry and protect the interests of the public and legitimate pharmaceutical companies (see Satchwell 2004: 19), the regulatory framework can become weakened as a direct result of specific *legal* trade practices. These include a number of regulatory and legal loopholes hampering the authorities' ability to tackle the real extent of the trade. The most common one relates to parallel trade. We discuss this in more detail in Chap. 4, including the most prominent case of illegal trading in medicines known to UK law enforcement, which involved the main actor posing as a parallel trader. In summary, this practice involves private traders in the EU legally passing large quantities of medicines through national economies with high-price markets in a quest for profit maximisation, which creates supply shortages in exporting countries. This opens up opportunities for illicit parallel traders to supply falsified medicinal products because the shortages create increased demand in the market (European Parliament 2011) and entry points through which smugglers can introduce illicit medicines into the legitimate pharmaceutical supply chain.

As we touched on in the last chapter, another broader issue weakening regulation and detection in the UK is the varied intellectual property and licensing laws that operate over different jurisdictional boundaries. A product deemed fake in one nation state may be legitimate in another. Suppliers of fakes exploit this in the knowledge that certain medicines produced outside the UK (sometimes legitimately) but sold in the UK do not pose as much of a legal risk. They may also operate their websites from outside the UK, which UK authorities are unable to regulate. For example, international online pharmacies and international online wholesalers can offer shipping and delivery to the UK and worldwide. These sites can essentially bypass the Medicines Act of 1968, which criminalises the selling of prescription drugs to customers who have no prescription, because the online sellers are aware this law can be enforced only if companies are UK-based and selling to UK consumers. Therefore, with no legal jurisdiction over production or distribution centres abroad, POMs can be supplied legally without prescription to UK consumers. This online trade also provides illicit drug producers and distributors with less risk and also higher profit margins as it offers the consumer both convenience and choice in the market.

Although it is currently illegal for any pharmaceutical supplier in the UK to advertise their products via direct-to-consumer advertising (DTCA), the Internet and, more specifically, Web 2.0—referring to the second generation of the Web with increased user-generated content—present abundant marketing and advertising opportunities for illicit suppliers (see Hall and Antonopoulos 2015). Therefore, the illegitimate online market for pharmaceuticals cannot be regulated in the same way as DTCA in the legitimate pharmaceutical industry (see Fox 2005a for a discussion of DTCA, which is currently illegal in the UK). Laing and Mackey (2011) call the recent availability of this drug advertising online 'eDTCA 2.0' and argue that this practice can circumvent legal exclusions and thus allow *forums and social networking sites to market specific drugs without any regulatory oversight*. Pfizer recently responded to this by offering a legitimate B2C path online direct to the consumer, selling Viagra through their website in a bid to beat the counterfeiters. This is the first known instance in which a pharmaceutical company has sold their products directly to consumers via the Internet in the UK.

Overall, what we have seen in this section are some examples of a whole spectrum of legal anomalies and loopholes that can render tackling the illicit medicine trade in the UK more difficult. The combination of relatively low risk and high profit margins makes this an attractive market for illicit suppliers in a variety of global locations.

THE INTERNET INFRASTRUCTURE

The following chapters discuss the demand-side and supply side in more detail, but first it is necessary to outline the virtual elements of the trade by exploring the facilitating roles played by late modern ICTs. Therefore, this section will discuss the Internet infrastructure required for this form of e-commerce, including the online platforms and services currently being used to market illicit medicines, as well as the detection-avoidance tactics adopted by cyber-criminal entrepreneurs involved in the trade (see also Hall and Antonopoulos 2015). The flexibility and anonymity inherent in this online environment highlights the continuous blurring between licit and illicit activities.

A variety of tools and services are required as a basic infrastructure for all e-commerce traders, including online illicit medicine suppliers. For example, the infrastructure of an illegal entrepreneur trading via an illicit online pharmacy will include a domain registrar, a counterfeit website, an Internet service provider (ISP) web host, a website template design, a download server and a payment service provider. The purchaser visits the counterfeit website informed by the marketing tactics we will describe in more detail shortly, which include sponsored ads, social media posts, search engine algorithmic results or spam messages (Anaman 2014). An obvious primary component of the infrastructure is an ISP. An ISP is an organisation that provides services for accessing or participating on the Internet. Some non-profit ISPs exist but most are commercial and privately owned (e.g. Virgin Media, BT and Sky in the UK).

However, more specifically, law enforcement agencies regard registrars, payment processors and payment gateways as the integral nodes of the infrastructure needed to trade in illicit medicines online, often referring to them as the 'choke points' of the process (Burke 2014). Adequate regulation of these points can result in the closure of illegal online pharmacies. Registrars are accredited by the Internet Corporation for Assigned Names and Numbers. They are commercial entities authorised to sell domain names to the public. A very popular example is *GoDaddy.com*. Registrars are compelled to follow the law in their everyday business and are obliged to shut down illegal online pharmacies by suspending and 'locking' the domain name, therefore, ensuring that it is not transferred to another member of the public. A registrar found to be accepting fees from known illegal online pharmacies is considered to be a participant in criminal activity. However, registrars respond to notifications from law enforcement authorities in various ways. Some cooperate, whereas others do not and are thus deemed *non-compliant registrars.*

A payment processor is a company, such as MasterCard or PayPal, which is appointed by a merchant to handle transactions for merchants. Payment processors enable the merchants to receive debit or credit card payments online by providing connections to their acquiring banks. These processors perform a number of functions, which include evaluating whether transactions are valid and approved, and providing anti-fraud measures to assure that a purchase transaction is initiated by the source it claims to be. Payment gateways are also essential. They send credit card transactions to the payment processors, who are appointed to handle transactions with the acquiring bank. Significantly, payment gateways encrypt merchant and customer information during e-commerce transactions and offer secure pages. During the research we were informed of one criminal organisation that owned and operated 2026 domain names using 75 similar website templates, provided by 36 domain registrars, hosted by 27 ISPs, leading to only 12 payment gateways. Similarly, the Pangea IV operation identified 1412 illegal online pharmacies, 928 of which led to payment pages. Of those, 649 websites (or approximately 70 %) were connected to only four payment pages (see Anaman 2014). These examples emphasise the presence of large-scale *concentrated* schemes involved in the online trade in illicit medicines. However, we have also found a range of tactics now being adopted to trade in illicit medicines online, which make use of various nodes in the infrastructure mentioned above.

The Platforms, Services and Tools Used to Market Illicit Medicines Online

Combining data from our virtual ethnography with data from law enforcement and private stakeholders, we found a number of platforms, services, tools and sites that are regularly used to market and advertise illicit medicines online. These include online marketplaces, peer-to-peer (P2P) networks, BitTorrent index/Tracker websites, one-click host downloads, online mail order and social media link-sharing/posts (Anaman 2014). Some of these are also used for communication between suppliers involved at various stages in the supply chain. The following sections categorise and describe the main B2B, B2C and C2C platforms and sites used to market illicit medicines online, although it is worth mentioning that they can require the use of a range of software and communications protocols.

Online Pharmacies
The primary sites for medicine supply online in the UK are Online Pharmacies (OPs). OPs are pharmacies that operate over the Internet and post their products to consumers via a shipping company or the postal service. In 1999 the first OP appeared in the UK, named Pharmacy2U. This service offered a range of medicines available to customers who could supply a doctor's note or private prescription (BBC Online 1999). This was not supported by the National Health Service (NHS), but since 2005 the NHS has developed an online prescription service of its own (see Fox and Ward 2006). Pharmacy2U is still in operation and offers prescription-only medicines after a free online consultation—a practice that can also present a number of risks, particularly those associated with the lack of thorough

face-to-face interactions with a trained healthcare professional with access to patients' medical records.

There are various types of OP, all with a disembodied global mode of operating that constantly blurs the distinction between legitimate and illegitimate trade. Other than legitimate OPs, which include well-known pharmacy chains' online subsidiaries and independent pharmacies' online sites set up to simplify the ordering process and compete with larger companies, a range of illegitimate pharmacies are in constant operation. Although concerns have been raised about the legitimate online pharmacy sector in the UK, there are far more concerns about the host of illegal OPs that supply pharmaceuticals outside legitimate healthcare channels.

A variety of indicators show whether OPs are acting outside the law. Most offer POMs without a prescription, whereas others offer forged online prescription services which simply ask the customer to 'virtually discuss' their supposed health concerns with someone posing as an online doctor. Some are transparently illegitimate on many fronts, yet still maintain a customer base. In the data we found countless OPs offering a quick, affordable option that did not require a prescription. Other obvious ways to tell if an OP is illegitimate is the concealment of its physical address and the webpage's connection to specific web-hosting services that are more likely to be implicated in the trade (see also LegitScript's top ten list). Moreover, a large percentage of illegal OPs that claim to be UK-based are based overseas in order to bypass the UK's legal restrictions. For example, the huge increase in online 'Canadian Pharmacies'—although of course the majority are not based in Canada—is the result of criminal actors recognising the opportunity presented by the rising popularity of Canadian drugs due to their relative affordability in comparison to American drugs (see DeKieffer 2006: 5). The 'Canadian Pharmacy' brand name is implicated in the operations of a large Russian-based criminal organisation and, as we discuss in more detail below, various forms of web manipulation can be used to hide the involvement of larger criminal groups involved in the supply chain.

In 2008 the UK introduced the green cross logo in order to offer legitimacy and help UK consumers identify authentic online pharmacies. However, some rogue pharmacies have attempted to plagiarise the logo on their sites. In addition, there is a free online service offered by LegitScript, a company that verifies and monitors OPs, whereby consumers can check the classification of an online pharmacy simply by entering the

OP's Uniform Resource Locator (URL) on their websites. LegitScript's classification system for OPs includes the categories of legitimate, rogue, unapproved or unverified. A rogue pharmacy is a site knowingly involved in drug distribution outside of law and regulation. Unverified is a 'neutral' term used to denote sites which have only been briefly reviewed, but seem to comply with standards. Unapproved pharmacies are not necessarily rogues but appear to lack some of the necessary legal and regulatory standards. Importantly, LegitScript include in their classification sites that directly supply 'a prescription drug or medical device' *and* sites that redirect to another for supply. Moreover, they apply the laws of the jurisdiction from where the site is operating *and* the applicable laws of the countries to which the sites offer shipping (see www.legitscript.com).

Via Google we identified websites claiming to be OPs offering prescription-only medicines without prescription delivered to UK addresses. Then we gathered data on their web-hosting company and whether or not the pharmacy's physical address was available. All of these are key indicators of illegal trading. During the course of the virtual ethnography a variety of styles and idiosyncrasies were found. Some sites were noticeably cheap and rogue. Most large-scale illegal OPs were found through a redirect from a page unrelated to the trade, followed by another redirect transferring the consumer to an online merchant trader to pay by credit card. However, we found instances where OPs offered payments via MoneyGram, PayPal or Western Union, some even direct into a seller's bank account. Some solely sold drugs used to treat ED, others a range of lifestyle and lifesaving drugs, and others were initial points of contact before email discussions were generated and full product/price lists offering an entire range of drugs, including pharmaceuticals and new research chemicals, were offered. These often included 'special deals' on large quantities of specific drugs and offered delivery options and 'agents available' in a number of nation states.

Using data from the NCA we pooled information from a database monitoring OPs. The following graph highlights the percentage of OPs selling to UK consumers using the same web-hosting company, indicating that the large majority use a variety of lesser-known web-hosting companies (categorised as 'other'; Fig. 2.2):

This next graph uses the same data set to highlight the percentage from the same list of OPs with no physical address, a key indicator of an OP acting illicitly (Fig. 2.3):

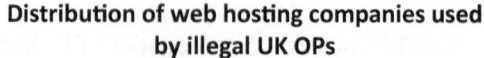

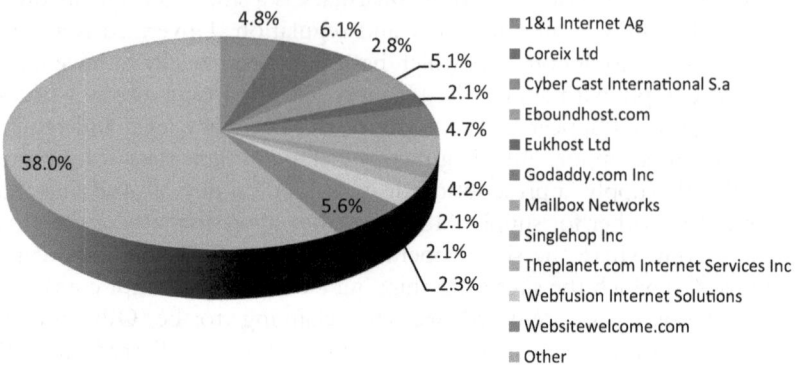

Fig. 2.2   Graph highlighting the distribution of web-hosting companies used by illegal online pharmacies (*Source*: UK National Crime Agency (NCA) 2014)

This is a hugely profitable business. In a conversation with UK law enforcement agencies specialising in the trade we were informed that domain names can be bought for as little as 69 cents. Larger criminal operations bulk buy domain names, usually with a contract from the website owners, for one year, to which they add similar templates. One product alone, sold through a variety of websites by a larger operation, has often returned £1.2 million in profit per month. Institute of Research Against Counterfeit Medicines (IRACM) also note (IRACM 2013: 18) that an investment of $1000 in the counterfeiting of a 'blockbuster drug'—that is, a medicine making profit of $1 billion or more legitimately for a pharmaceutical company—can secure a return of $500,000. This is much more profitable than heroin or cocaine and presents far less risk of prosecution.

'Pandora's (In)Box: Email, Spam and Web Manipulation
Email also plays an essential role in the illicit online medicine trade. Often a relationship between buyer and seller forged via an OP or social media site is maintained in a subsequent email discussion. During the ethnographic research numerous introductions to sellers made via social media were continued by email discussion. Many claimed to be based in the UK, Pakistan or USA, and offered a wide range of drugs, including pharmaceuticals,

Percentage of OPs with or without registered physical address

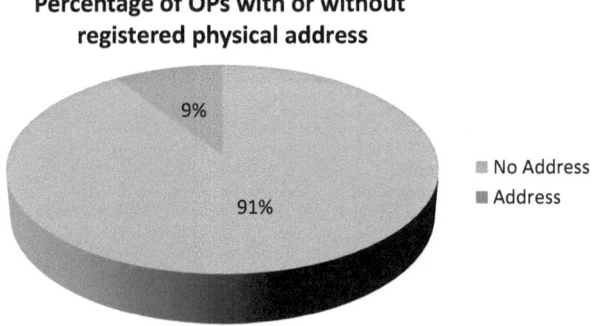

Fig. 2.3   Graph highlighting the percentage of online pharmacies with or without a physical address (*Source*: UK National Crime Agency (NCA) 2014)

new research chemicals and more well-known illicit chemicals used recreationally (ketamine, GBH, etc.). Consumers and suppliers online also mentioned the use of Hushmail accounts—a service offering Pretty Good Privacy (PGP) encrypted email—as a means of continuing business relationships with heightened anonymity.

Another way illicit pharmaceutical suppliers promote their business and merchandise online is through the use of spam emails. Spam email directly offering pharmaceutical products is widespread, particularly drugs to treat ED—one of the most in-demand online products in the UK. Some spam emails are used to send links to OPs or details of a seller directly. One of the most prolific counterfeit medicine traders online known to the authorities is the Russian-based GlavMed, which has been described as 'one of the most significant cases of cybercrime in the pharmaceutical sector' (IRACM 2013: 70). They run their online pharmacy operation alongside their large spam company SpamIt. According to M86 Security Labs, the sites advertised in GlavMed/SpamIt emails—best known by their 'Canadian Pharmacy' brand name—were by far the most prevalent affiliate brands promoted by spam as of June 2010 (Krebs on Security 2011; see Fig. 2.4). In addition, after researching 218 drug-related queries over nine months in 2010–2011, cybersecurity researchers at Carnegie Mellon University found that illegal pharmacies use spam emails to manipulate web search results and promote their business (Medical Daily 2011).

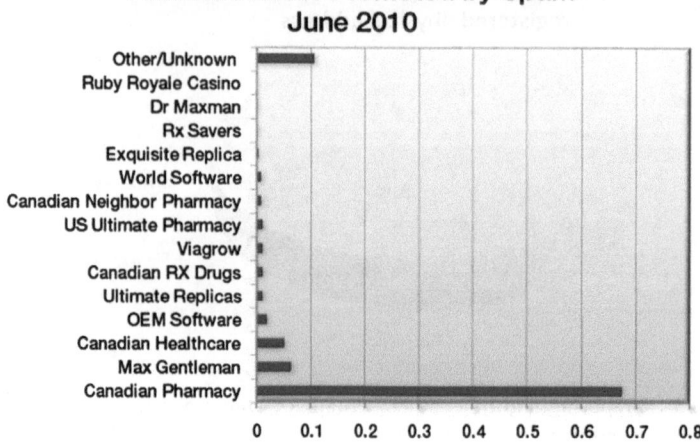

Fig. 2.4 Affiliate brands promoted by spam, June 2010 (*Source*: Krebs on Security (2011))

The practice of using spam emails has been used—primarily by illegal entrepreneurs with the highest IT literacy—in conjunction with another practice: web manipulation. This method has been viewed as far more efficient than spam emails. As the lead researcher of the project at Carnegie Mellon University noted, 'unauthorised online pharmacies have been using e-mail spam to tap the wallets of unwary online consumers but that method did not blanket enough customers so now [the illegal entrepreneurs] are infecting websites to redirect unwary consumers to hundreds of illegal online pharmacies' (Science Daily 2011). Specifically, they found that one-third of their collected search results during the study—7000 infected websites—triggered an active redirect to a few hundred illegal online pharmacies sites. Affiliate and sub-affiliate networks often play a crucial role in this process. An affiliate network is constructed in two ways:

1. By entrepreneurs who are responsible for a number of websites illegally trading in medicines; often the websites have a very similar if not identical template.
2. By the use of 'affiliates', whereby larger 'organisations' operating OPs pay commercial entities commission to surf the web and 'set up clone pages mimicking the website of the "spider" and/or merely post a URL link' on their site to the pharmacy. In other words, indi-

viduals or affiliate programs run by individuals post links to OPs on various online sites and are paid for each 'customer who has "clicked through" the affiliate's link'. (DeKieffer 2006: 9)

These networks provide a crucial marketing function as well as rendering detection more difficult.

Social Media Sites
In a recent presentation a law enforcement agent working for the MHRA argued that 'social media is the new spam' (Truick 2014). Our online research supports the claim that the use of social media link-sharing and posting by illicit medicine traders is on the increase. The online ethnographic research revealed numerous examples where social media sites, particularly Facebook, were used as online sites for supply (see Hansson et al. 2013; Vance et al. 2009; Su and Holt 2010; Huang et al. 2011; Banyai and Glover 2012; van Hellemont 2012; He et al. 2013; Post et al. 2013 for the use of social media in several industries and research projects). Connections between seller and buyer were forged via friends' lists and Facebook groups affiliated to prescription drugs or linked to subcultures wherein prescription drug use is prevalent. Friends tend to post stock available directly on their walls or on the page of a group, often with photographic evidence of the product alongside their names and the date. Virtual 'word of mouth' can play an important role in terms of establishing, assuring and circulating the legitimacy of a seller and quality of the service on offer, especially as users are concerned about becoming victims of 'scams' and subsequently being defrauded.

Some actors used a variety of social networking sites to advertise their products. We found evidence of opioids and ED drugs for sale via sellers who post on sites such as Instagram and Twitter. Successful sales often depend on a number of users who are critically positioned in a network (see Jürgens et al. 2011). As we explore in more detail in Chap. 3, participatory web cultures and social media sites allow for a process of *prosumption* in fake pharmaceutical trading, where often there is no clear demarcation between the producer, trader and consumer involved in marketing and advertising illicit medicines. This, we are convinced, is evidence of a cultural shift in general consumption habits. The online market in illicit pharmaceuticals is an important example of this shift as growing numbers of people become active users generating content online via social media websites.

Furthermore, there is an abundance of marketing research suggesting that consumers are heavily influenced by Internet-based forums before they make purchasing decisions (Dellarocas 2006). Therefore, entrepreneurs exploit discussions in online forums in the knowledge that potential customers tend to be more interested in a product if it is perceived as 'authentically' endorsed, rather than a product purposefully promoted by marketer-generated sources (Bickart and Schindler 2001). In a similar vein, online forums have been identified as critical and strategic discussion platforms facilitating what Woerndl et al. (2008) call 'viral marketing': transmitting messages and information about products quickly to a wide audience. This can be manipulated by criminals involved in the trade who pose as consumers, or more directly via the use of affiliates. It also confirms that production and consumption are involved in a process of co-creation in the context of participatory web cultures and pharmaceutical trading. Virtual specialised forums are not only spaces in which illegal entrepreneurs identify (and persuade) potential customers to purchase medicines for medical conditions that concern them, but also in which customers often collectively discuss their pharmaceutical consumption online without such persuasion. Forums have also emerged in the form of what Soudijn and Zegers (2012) call 'convergence setting' for criminals; locations in which potential collaborators may meet one another. Hence, Internet-based forums—in an increasingly normalised process of time/space compression—provide access to large numbers of consumers situated globally *and* offer opportunities for criminal entrepreneurs to connect with one another.

Online Wholesalers and Classified Advertising

We found two specific online marketplaces based in Asia selling large quantities of chemicals, materials, equipment and finished medicinal products to UK distributors and consumers. These products are attempting to bypass IP laws and are therefore deemed as fake. These sites offer B2B and direct B2C platforms for trade in illicit medicines.

Alibaba is one of the largest e-commerce markets in the world, so big that in 2012 the site processed the selling of more goods than Amazon and eBay combined (The Economist 2013a, b). This particular e-commerce company, which operates B2B, B2C and C2C services, has been defined as the 'champion for the little guy. Alibaba largely served the small manufacturing business in China, making it easy for them to connect with overseas buyers' (Feng 2013: 9). However, Alibaba is rife with counterfeit products. We found large quantities of powdered APIs under their generic names. For example, Zopiclone, a non-benzodiazepine, which is a patented product with Sanofi Aventis for sale in the UK, was being sold in powdered form in 200 kilo quantities direct from a chemical company based in mainland China. Furthermore, the equipment needed to press pills at home was also for sale.

TradeIndia, an online Indian-based B2B portal, was another large online marketplace illegitimately offering direct sales of pharmaceutical products under patent in the UK. We found direct evidence of a seller on Facebook who was supplied by a TradeIndia seller (see Chap. 3). In this case the ingredients/chemicals, pressing and packaging were being supplied to small clandestine operations based in the UK.

Furthermore, we found classified advertising via such sites as Craigslist being used to sell smaller quantities of illicit medicines. We found Oxycontin, Ritalin and Percocet among others for sale, mainly in the 'Health and Beauty' section. A variety of other sites posing as UK-based online pharmaceutical wholesalers offered 'special products', which suggests that goods and services lying at the margins of legitimacy are being advertised.

Darknet Markets

There has been quite a lot of discussion in the UK media regarding the Silk Road, an unregulated US-based online marketplace recently seized by the FBI (see GQ 2013; Ball 2013). Silk Road was a hyper-libertarian vision of online trading set up by a self-proclaimed anarcho-capitalist who professed to be anti-state and anti-regulation. The Internet presents ample opportunities for individuals like this who prefer the unregulated shadow economy because it allows them to develop high levels of sophistication and continuously groundbreaking marketing techniques. This is one example of a darknet market or cryptomarket (see Martin 2014) operating on the *dark web*, which is part of the broader *deep web*. These darknet operations or 'darknets' use overlay networks that can be accessed only by using specific software designed to offer further anonymity to buyers and sellers. This offers a near-perfect opportunity for dealers of contraband and largely illicit pharmaceutical drugs to trade online with lower risk of detection. According to Christin (2012), who conducted a measurement analysis of Silk Road, 16.8 per cent of items in the top 20 category ordered via this particular marketplace were pharmaceutical products including 'prescription drugs', 'steroids' and 'benzos'. This is something enforcement agencies suspect will proliferate over time.

These 'anonymous' networks with layered encryption are more difficult for authorities to monitor. Two of the largest networks operating on the dark web are Invisible Internet Project and Tor. Tor, an acronym for The Onion Router, is designed for online anonymity and offers layered encryption to buyers and sellers. It is a network designed to pass IP addresses and web transactions through numerous relays, using random and anonymised URLs in order to conceal users' locations and Internet activities. Once Tor is accessed, a buyer and seller can trade in various digital currencies, such as Bitcoin, and use data encryption and decryption tools, for example, PGP encryption, to encrypt and decrypt messages. This has provided distributors of drugs a relatively anonymous and unregulated online marketplace. Darknets can also include P2P networks, which are also heavily implicated in the illicit medicine trade (see Anaman 2014). Our research has found numerous sellers of prescription-only medicines, steroids and other illicit drugs on the dark web across various darknet marketplaces.

Online Detection-Avoidance Tactics

Illegal entrepreneurs also use a number of digital techniques to avoid law enforcement and health regulatory agencies' efforts to close them down. Firstly, as mentioned earlier, darknets can offer heightened anonymity for suppliers and consumers: they cannot be indexed by search engines, they use data encryption services and they use networks designed to move data relating to buyers' and sellers' locations around a number of intermediaries. Attempting to monitor operations on the dark web is particularly time-consuming and requires a relatively high level of IT skill. As technical anonymisation operations become more sophisticated the bar is constantly raised, which of course means that monitoring is becoming increasingly difficult for authorities who are always at least one step behind. Secondly, affiliate and sub-affiliate networks (see discussion above) are also used to 'muddy the waters'. These networks are used by illicit operations to spread their online reach by displaying large numbers of websites acting as OPs with similar or identical templates. Thirdly, illegal entrepreneurs buy their domains from 'rogue registrars', such as *TodayNIC, BizCN, WebNIC.cc., Joker.com, IPMirror* and others. These non-compliant registrars tend to ignore law enforcement and regulatory agencies' requests to block and shut down specific sites deemed to be associated with the illegal sale of medicines.

Fourthly, illegal entrepreneurs engage in something similar to counterintelligence. They attempt to identify unusual patterns of 'behaviour' on the part of law enforcement and health regulatory agents posing as customers. Specifically, they check the details of visitors to their affiliate sites, including the frequency of visits and the debit/credit card used for purchases. If a visitor is found to be making a number of visits to a number of their affiliate sites, as well as using the same card for payment, this is an indication of a law enforcement officer or health regulatory agent monitoring the website and/or conducting test purchases. If the illegal entrepreneurs identify such 'unusual' behaviour from the 'fingerprint' (IP address), the 'potential client' is blocked or re-directed to another website (e.g. back to Google or to a site unrelated to the pharmaceutical industry).

Fifthly, illegal entrepreneurs actively attempt to avoid the WHOIS check that is performed by law enforcement authorities and regulatory agencies in order to identify illegal online pharmacies. WHOIS checks the following:

1. The company acting as the 'registrar'.
2. The registrant of the domain name (basically the company or individual who has bought the domain name).
3. The registration date.
4. The IP address.
5. The company address.

Law enforcement and health regulatory agents use WHOIS services provided by websites such as *www.domaintools.com*. According to the PFIPC (2014), it can be extremely difficult to track the ultimate source of a website because many of the major illegal pharmacies—in a process similar to the one associated with the use of overlay networks on the dark web—use 'fast flux' in order to hide their physical location:

> The simplest type of 'fast flux', referred to as 'single-flux', is characterised by multiple individual nodes within the network registering and de-registering their addresses for a single DNS (Domain Name System) name. This creates a constantly changing list of destination addresses for that single DNS name – perhaps as often as every three minutes. The list can be hundreds or thousands of entries long. (PFIPC 2014: 14)

Sixthly, criminal entrepreneurs reroute payments through intermediaries and thus obfuscate the relationships existing between illegal activities and payments (see Burke 2014). Law enforcement and health regulatory agencies consider 'following the money' as a reliable way of identifying illegal entrepreneurs involved in the illicit pharmaceutical trade. Indeed, 'following the money' is regarded as a way of counterbalancing the limitations of other aspects of the criminal investigation and a way of targeting the most important actors involved in a pharmaceutical crime network. However, illegal entrepreneurs largely avoid asking for bank payments because, on occasion, according to MHRA agents, the name of the beneficiary can be obtained from the transaction's paper trail. Instead, entrepreneurs prefer money transfer services (such as Western Union) because they are extremely easy to use, and, at least for smaller transactions, no identification is required. In addition, illegal entrepreneurs forge multiple banking relationships in numerous ways. They have been known to ask family members, friends and/or acquaintances to borrow their accounts for a number of transactions, or they have rented the accounts of others for a short time. In Chap. 4 we discuss a case that offers a definitive illustration of a network of friends and family members involved in the illicit medicine trade who forged multiple banking relationships. Moreover, digital currencies are increasingly being used, offering further concealment for traders and compounded difficulties for law enforcement.

Conclusion

This chapter has explored the history of pharmaceutical falsification, how digital technologies increasingly facilitate the trade in illicit medicines and the specific dynamics of the UK market. The trade in illicit medicines is a growing phenomenon with an extensive history. However, a number of legal loopholes existing alongside political, economic and technological shifts in the late twentieth and early twenty-first century have laid down the conditions for vast market growth. As this chapter has shown, the UK's role in the trade is best understood as both a transit zone and end-user market. As an end-user market most medicines are available online to UK consumers. However, lifestyle medicines make up the majority of those bought by the UK consumer via illicit sites.

Various nodes in the Internet infrastructure facilitate the techniques currently being developed by criminal entrepreneurs trading in illicit medicines. Online suppliers of illicit medicines use a range of sites—often simultaneously—to target their market sectors and advertise their products and prices to consumers. These include online pharmacies, social media sites, online wholesalers' sites, classified advertising sites, email and spam, online forums and darknet markets found on the deep web. We have found that affiliate and sub-affiliate networks can play crucial roles in marketing illicit medicines online by providing greater market reach and avoiding detection by obscuring individual market operations. Furthermore, cyber-criminal entrepreneurs who supply illicit medicines use a range of other common detection-avoidance practices. As we have shown, they choose non-compliant registrars to access domain names, monitor the behaviour of visitors to their sites, circumvent the WHOIS protocol and reroute payments.

CHAPTER 3

The Demand Side

Abstract This chapter explores the cultural and technological factors contributing to the growing consumption of illicit medicines bought online. First it contextualises the UK consumer/patient in the virtual world. Next, drawing on ethnographic research data, it offers an advanced understanding of the consumer decision-making processes and other contributing factors that influence the purchase of medicines online. Finally, it reveals the social groups most at risk of buying and consuming illicit medicines online in the UK. Distribution of illicit medicines to these groups is theorised in the broad contexts of (1) changing cultures of pharmaceutical consumption and healthcare practice and (2) the effects of digital technologies operating in broader politico-economic structures and processes.

Keywords demand • consumer/patient • lifestyle medicines • steroids • recreational drug use

In a country with a functioning National Health Service (NHS), the UK consumer's move to the Internet to buy illicit medicines offers a prescient example of consumer culture as a context for profound shifts in late-modern identity and cultural practices, yet it remains under-researched. This chapter sets out to empirically and theoretically investigate the consumer demand for illicit medicines online in the UK and highlight specific

© The Author(s) 2016
A. Hall, G.A. Antonopoulos, *Fake Meds Online*,
DOI 10.1057/978-1-137-57088-8_3

types of deviance and risk. The chapter will answer the following research questions, which have been formulated in order to achieve these aims:

- What are the dynamics and key determinant factors shaping pharmaceutical consumption online in the UK?
- What impact does this have on the trade in illicit medicines?
- What type of networks and patterns inform this process virtually, socially and culturally?
- Which social groups are more at risk of consuming illicit medicines?

Overall, the chapter will offer an advanced understanding of the consumer decision-making processes and other contributing factors that influence the purchase of medicines online, and it will highlight who is at risk of buying and consuming illicit medicines. Following a preliminary contextualisation of the UK consumer/patient, late-modern health practices, the virtual world and illicit medicines, examples from the virtual and offline ethnographies will be used as case studies. These will highlight this cultural shift in detail, and also show how specific medicines, modes of communication in forums and social networking sites, and a range of other factors contribute to the purchase of various illicit medicines online. This data-driven analysis is contextualised in a theoretical discussion of the effects of digital technologies operating in broader politico-economic structures and processes and in changing cultures of pharmaceutical consumption and healthcare practice.

Although most studies focus on supply, an exploration of the demand side begs a number of equally important research questions. For instance, how and why does the sociocultural and political-economic climate in the UK impact on both the availability of illicit medicines online and the ultimate decision to buy them rather than use the NHS? How has the rise of the Internet and modernisation of the 'user-led' NHS interacted to push the so-called self-diagnosing 'expert patient' towards online methods for healthcare and away from professionals? Are the majority of consumers buying medicines online unable to obtain prescriptions, which also increases the risk of consuming potentially dangerous illicit medicines? Furthermore, what are consumers' attitudes towards illicit pharmaceuticals? Do they suggest a distrust of large pharmaceutical companies or the healthcare system, or are self-diagnosis and the purchasing of medicines online merely becoming an accepted aspect of everyday consumption patterns?

Pharmaceutical Drugs, the Internet and the UK Consumer

The Internet facilitates the social connection of various communities in diverse and dispersed locations. Buyer and seller never have to meet and, with discretion at a premium, tend to engage in brief communications. Therefore, abstract factors such as variegated regulations and price differentials—which in some instances can be as high as 16:1 for pharmaceuticals with expired patents—as well as the corresponding affordability, coverage decisions and availability of specific medicines (see European Parliament 2011; see also Mossialos et al. 2004) tend to have determinant impacts on the mechanisms of the online global trade in illicit pharmaceuticals. Data relating to seizures of illicit medicines offer some insights into the main products currently supplied and where they are produced (see Bates 2008: 8; Chaps. 2, 4). However, in order to understand the largely under-researched consumer demand side for medicines specifically being traded online requires an in-depth analysis that drills down into the underlying motivations for consumption and the relationship between pharmaceuticals and the Internet.

Walsh (2011) argues that drugs and the Internet have a symbiotic relationship in terms of their cultural effects, and that since its inception the Internet has been exploited by those involved in drug distribution: 'Facilitating consumerism, the Internet is a medium through which "white," "grey" and "black" drug markets flourish, with the boundaries between them shifting and amorphous, fluid and arbitrary' (Walsh 2011: 56). However, researching the virtual world and drug distribution is fraught with difficulties. Online flows of information are vast and constant, IP addresses are hidden, and fraudulent and anonymous identities abound. As Chap. 5 shows, there is now an increasing role being played by the 'invisible', 'dark' or 'deep' web with its layered encryption that is more difficult for authorities to monitor (see Martin 2014).

However, these activities are not limited to the darknet; they are also evident on the surface web, where the majority of consumers buy products. Since its establishment across the globe in the 1990s, the Internet has assisted both B2B and direct B2C transactions. Both legitimate and illegitimate trade in pharmaceuticals have benefitted from this development. As we have pointed out, a simple search for a generic substance on Alibaba.com or TradeIndia.com can result in large wholesale quantities being shipped to your door from China or South Asia. Online pharmacies, social networking sites, unsolicited emails and classified advertising also publicise medicines for sale without prescription, and an array of forums normalise prescription drug taking and buying online in discussions and accumulated information dispersed throughout their networks. Therefore, the structures of the legitimate and illegitimate online trade in pharmaceuticals are not distinct, and the specific politico-economic and cultural processes that have encouraged a shift in the UK-based healthcare practices and pharmaceutical consumption to online methods provide the main context in which our analysis of the demand side must be contextualised.

Web 2.0 and the Privatisation of Healthcare

There was a shift in patterns of production and consumption towards the end of the twentieth century after a period of deindustrialisation and deregulation precipitated a shift in the balance from a productive to a consumer-service economy. Neoliberal policies not only sought to deregulate markets and privatise public services but also to realise in these processes and new conditions a 'consumerist vision of the world'. This vision, as Smart (2010: 39) notes,

> effectively elevates the consumer to sovereign status, possessing freedom and exercising unimpaired choice, not only in the commercial marketplace, where the pursuit of private interest has long held sway, but increasingly within the public sector, where privatization policies and the imposition of internal markets or quasi-market mechanisms, misleadingly represented as 'modernization', have been accompanied by political rhetoric extolling the presumed benefits to be gained by an extension of 'consumer choice' to health and education provision in particular.

Under New Labour (1997–2010) this was articulated in their reform and 'modernisation' of the NHS, and culturally reinforced with the rhetoric of 'the consumer' rather than 'the patient'. Under the current British government this has been further intensified. The current changes being put into practice in the UK by the Conservative Party involve a vast privatisation of the health service, with the Health and Social Care bill currently being amended to introduce competition 'into almost every NHS activity' (Reynolds et al. 2012: 215; Wright 2012; see also Whitehead and Antonopoulos 2014). In many ways the Internet has assisted this move.

Fox et al. (2005a) point to three 'moments' in the development of 'Internet-facilitated pharmacy' in the UK that have helped give rise to the current medicalisation of everyday life and the normalisation of the customer's search for solutions to health matters online:

1. *Electronic transfer of prescription*—being delivered in two stages this enables the electronic transfer of prescriptions from doctor to pharmacist and highlights the move to modernise the NHS through ICT.
2. *E-pharmacy and the 'virtual' pharmacist*—this represents the development of legitimate online pharmacies, whereby patients complete a questionnaire which is then verified by a trained pharmacist to access prescription-only medicines (POMs).
3. *The E-clinic and the virtual prescriber*—this relates to establishing 'the online medical consultation as an alternative model for prescribing' and dispensing POMs.

The third 'moment' is often regarded as the most 'radical break with traditional modes of accessing POMs in the UK' (ibid, n.p.), mainly because no direct meeting with a healthcare provider is necessary. Accompanied by the discursive shift away from 'patient' towards 'consumer', it includes an 'un-moderated forum that allows consumers to discuss treatments directly with each other, independent of medical intervention' (ibid, n.p.).

The whole process as described earlier has been enhanced by user-generated content on social networking sites, 'where users are increasingly involved in *creating* web content as well as *consuming* it' (Beer and Burrows 2007; emphasis in original). With the rise of Web 2.0, the once distinct roles of producers and consumers have been somewhat blurred as they have become influenced by the participatory nature of virtual/social interaction (see Ritzer and Jurgenson 2010). Beer and Burrows (2010) discuss the participatory and active roles consumers now take in these spaces of consumption. For example, forums, blogs and social networking sites allow the exchange of information and network formation between individuals who then share their consumption practices. As Sassatelli notes, 'electronic commerce requires consumers to be much more active than anticipated' (2007: 166).

Alvin Toffler (1980) argued that post-industrial society bears witness to a 'reintegration' of the once separate spheres of production and consumption to a knowledge-producing era of the *prosumer*—a term used to deny the 'false binary' between production and consumption, where instead they are seen to be unified in a process of 'co-creation'. Whereas Smart

(2010) is not keen on the label, and critical of Toffler's expectation that prosumption would accompany an end to market economics, he supports his analysis that ICT has changed the nature and dynamics of production and consumption. However, for Smart this process has further increased the 'encroachment of the market into more and more areas of people's lives' (Smart 2010: 22). As the above highlights and we will see below when we discuss key causal factors, our examples of pharmaceutical technologies and consumption have also changed as a result of e-commerce and Web 2.0, by involving the consumer more actively, blurring processes of production and consumption, and privatising trade relationships. McDonald and Wearing see this process as a form of estrangement, whereby 'products and services are bought and sold in a sphere of anonymity' (2013: 103). The advent of e-commerce or the 'third market', alongside the privatisation of the NHS and the increase in patient-led services, has further normalised a privatised relationship between consumer/patient and pharmaceutical producer. The Internet facilitates this 'disembeddedness' (see McDonald and Wearing 2013: 104), compressing time/space expanses and opening up and multiplying the possibilities for the consumption of illicit medicines with all their associated risks. However, the shift in the illicit medicine trade's embeddedness because of the role played by digital technologies is complex because a process of 'reintermediation' is also in train, with large Internet trading companies such as Google, Facebook and PayPal implicated in the trade (Guarnieri and Przyswa 2013), not to mention the significant role played by payment gateways and acquiring banks. The blurring of legitimate and illegitimate is quite obvious in many respects. Therefore, is this really an example of 'disembeddedness' or is it rather the reconstitution and further marketisation of everyday pharmaceutical consumption facilitated by communicative capitalism (see Dean 2005, 2009)?

Furthermore, these arguments above relate to legitimate healthcare practices and sites in the UK, yet these developments are also mirrored in less regulated and illegitimate sites specialising in pharmaceutical consumption, which have also opened up opportunities for counterfeiters and illicit traders and leave consumer/patients at greater risk of consuming illicit medicines. The following example is one of many from bodybuilding forums where users advertise and share experiences of sites to purchase POMs or banned substances online—in this case Xenical but many others relate to anabolic steroids:

Just look it up on the net, you can get it easily. You can get it from
*********, just to give one example.

Thus, the participatory nature of Web 2.0 has simultaneously encouraged and exploited the privatisation of healthcare practices and created further opportunities for trade in illicit medicines.

Alongside the more obvious adverse health effects there are other risks for the consumer to weigh up. For instance, there is the risk that products will be intercepted. Moreover, sites can often be traps set up to defraud customers of money, credit card details or other identity-related crimes. It is also difficult to ascertain who is a 'legitimate' supplier, the main reason why participatory networking sites, acting as a sort of virtual 'word of mouth', are also visited by consumers seeking to distinguish between sites or sellers involved in the (il)legitimate pharmaceutical trade and the fraudulent operators. These sites are used to share—amongst networks of individual users—information on the trustworthiness of a supplier, most frequently designated as a 'legit seller'. By 'legit seller' users are referring to an online drug dealer whose intention is to deliver the product they advertise, rather than a 'scammer' attempting to defraud the customer of money and/or illegally obtain personal details. Here we are looking at the organic cultural evolution of a language representing distinct shades of illegality rather than the legal/illegal dichotomy, which again indicates the cultural normalisation of illicit markets.

During the ethnography a group of consumer/suppliers on Facebook—users who were involved in both the distribution and the consumption of illicit POMs—acted to market each other and their products. The researchers were asked by users with similar 'friends' lists affiliated to the illegal pharmaceutical trade to recommend 'legit sellers'. Furthermore, the researchers' forum posts indicated that they were seeking a legitimate seller, from which followed private messages and emails discussing product ranges, prices and delivery details. Social networking therefore acts to market a 'legitimate' supplier on Facebook, who is in reality a supplier involved in the illegal trade of medicines who can be relied upon to ship the product they are advertising. These sites introduce consumer and supplier, from which email discussions follow whereby orders and details are exchanged and relationships established and, if satisfactory, continued.

As the virtual ethnographic research proceeded through its early stages it became apparent that the Internet can be conceptualised as a *non-place* (see Augé 1995; Winlow and Hall 2013) with user-led content created solely by those involved in production, supply and consumption. For example, we found the Facebook friend who consumes, markets and sells medicines bought in wholesale quantities from TradeIndia and also advertises the efficiency and trustworthiness of his wholesale supplier online:

> Trade India, glad I made myself a member some 5 yrs ago now, real trade, always comes through no matter how much the amount. 30000. Boom. On time, c.o.d. trust is precious in the game

In a conversation we had with the same individual, the supplier's own consumption became apparent:

Researcher: How do you want the cash?
Supplier: Either into my bank or w.union pal. Due not like lorazepam, 2 mil, there brilliant pal [sic]
Researcher: Never really had them. What's better about them? They cheaper?
Supplier: No there dearer if owt but personally I hate that taste the morning after, from zoppies I mean. Will you want zopiclone again? As I'll get some in ok [sic].

The entire process of supply, from wholesale to retail, is accomplished online, in many cases essentially bypassing those criminal brokers involved in the trade who operate via online pharmacies. Consumers also have the option of joining dedicated groups on social networking sites, set up to discuss specific medicines and sellers. Sellers often upload photographs of their products alongside a note of their name and the date as a way of proving their authenticity. Here Web 2.0 is a reiteration of prosumption with user-generated content, where late-modern consumer practices in simulated non-places involve consumers in a production and marketing process that is changing the spaces and patterns of consumption. Production and consumption are co-created as user-led services market and advertise products freely.

In summary, the current context of rapid developments in ICT and the privatisation of healthcare—in which consumption patterns are moving online, consumers share content and participate in their healthcare and drug practices, and a discourse of privatisation in health services is ascendant—has encouraged online consumption of medicines and opened up opportunities for illegitimate sites for pharmaceutical consumption. But how can we begin to more fully understand the motivations behind the purchase of pharmaceuticals online? Which social and cultural processes and practices account for the emergence, shape and dynamics of the electronic technologies being used to trade in illicit medicines? How do these patterns relate to broader healthcare systems and practices? What are the motivations behind consumers in the UK who buy these products online and put themselves at risk? Drawing on empirical data, various contributing factors will be explored. We will then examine the demographic characteristics of these consumers in order to analyse the specific individuals and social groups most at risk of consuming illicit medicines.

CONTRIBUTING FACTORS AND DEMOGRAPHIC VARIABLES

It is extremely easy to attempt to buy POMs online without prescription. As Chap. 2 suggested, online pharmacies, Facebook messages, email, forum chat and classified advertising offer many of the prescription drugs requested and individual suppliers frequently offer a large variety. The following is a summary of one forum entry that describes a user's experience during a two-year period of buying POMs online without prescription. This depicts a typical experience of a UK consumer we found during the ethnographic data gathering, who was buying medicines online and therefore at risk of consuming fakes. This offers an introductory empirical overview of the demand side (for ethical reasons the authors have summarised and anonymised this section):

> The individual is an on/off prescription drug addict who used online pharmacies as the sole source of their online drug supply over a three year period. After searching the web they discovered an online forum dedicated to online pharmacy reviews and became a regular member there. Through conversation on the forum they gained access to a private, invite only, forum discussion, which offered information on 'elite, backroom' sellers. They started buying Tramadol from an OP in which a completed questionnaire was required, who then posted the medicine overnight. The buyer then began using several of these pharmacies intermittently to feed their growing habit. They then moved to international online pharmacies (IOPs) in order to buy stronger opioid painkillers. The user wasn't sure if they had ever bought and consumed counterfeit drugs, but that they all seemed to contain the correct active ingredients either way. Forums discussed 'bad pills' and reviewed the effects and preference of generic or branded drugs. They had bought psychostimulants usually prescribed for ADHD from an IOP based in Asia that visually appeared to be counterfeit but had the intended effect. They mention the various payment processors used for payment to suppli-

ers. Finally they moved to what is referred to in forums as BIPs (Blatantly Illegal Pharmacies), which use similar templates as websites, yet most trade was done over email using hushmail accounts after an initial order had been made via the website. Interestingly, they said that they all seemed like they were 'run by the same organisation'. Through these means, although more expensive, all POs were available via next day delivery. Once initiated as a consumer over email, the name of payment receivers in various countries were given and Western Union used to make payment directly. The user describes feeling their behavior felt 'more illegal' once they started buying from BIOP and 'feeling nervous' when they collected packages from the Postal collection office.

The above is typical of many cases of online pharmaceutical consumption revealed by the ethnographic research. It demonstrates the variety of the sites offering supply and suggests that the reasons for purchase are more than simply price, including non-medical factors that can influence prescription drug (mis)use. It also emphasises the role networks and inside knowledge gathered online can play in the process, and demonstrates that variegated sites can often be run by the same criminal organisation (see Chap. 4). Moreover, it highlights this particular online pharmaceutical consumer's increased awareness that their behaviour was becoming increasingly deviant as the online sites for their consumption became less legitimate over time. The following section will discuss in more depth the key determinant factors we found in operation during the ethnographies.

Determinant Factors

Fox et al. (2005b) argue that the move to online methods for pharmaceutical distribution and consumption has been 'driven in part by commercial pressures in North America' and the private healthcare system there (2005b: 1474). The American example offers a particular case study in which consumers, burdened by the misinformation and costs of the private healthcare system, are attracted to the free information and affordability of medicines online sites provide. Yar also sees the '(neo)liberalisation of health care' as one of the main drivers of the growth in counterfeit pharmaceuticals (2008: 159). However, the impacts of processes of neoliberalisation or marketisation on the UK health practices are rather more complex. The NHS offers a fixed price for prescriptions—currently set at £7.10—and a prepayment certificate, which offers anyone the opportunity to obtain all of their legitimately prescribed medicines for £2 per week. Furthermore, if the individual falls into a variety of social categories relating to age, pregnancy and income-related support, he or she is entitled to free prescriptions. However, despite this subsidy there is still a burgeoning market in, and therefore demand for, online pharmaceuticals outside of legitimate healthcare structures, which points to reasons beyond price.

There are obvious cultural reasons behind this consumer move, some of which will also be argued here to be the results of neoliberalisation. In other words, the ideological reach of this politico-economic project moves beyond economic structures (such as trade practices or price differentials). It systematically pervades everyday life, its subjectivities and its culture; from feelings of inadequacy and insecurity (Hall et al. 2008), to a lack of trust in healthcare professionals and hyper-individualised health practices (Smart 2010). Along with convenience and availability, a range of crucial yet fluid, determining factors—which depend on the specific medication being consumed and the intended purpose—appear to be encouraging the individual to engage in deviant pharmaceutical drug purchasing online.

The Privatisation of Health Practices and the New Cultural Norm of the Consumer/Patient

As we have seen, cultural changes in consumption, the rise of Web 2.0 and market-based reform of the NHS have all interacted to effect significant change in healthcare practices in the UK. As Yar points out, in the UK:

> [A]s pressures toward privatization of healthcare increase, and the public health sector is subjected to marketisation, we may expect an expansion of opportunities and structures for counterfeits to enter legitimate supply chains (2008: 160)

This privatisation acts ideologically to inculcate in patients their pursuit of healthcare *on their own terms*, without face-to-face interaction and without the advice of trained professionals. Essentially, privatising the relationship between consumer/patient and pharmaceutical producer/supplier has increased demand for these products from online suppliers offering them without prescription, the most common practice on the sites where the largest quantities of illicit medicines are sold. As Jackson et al. note, 'patients are often unaware that they are buying counterfeit products or of the risks to which they are exposed' (2012). However, for some, the desire to consume these products often overrides their knowledge of the risks involved in consuming fakes.

The privatisation of the NHS and their campaigns for an 'expert patient' or 'patient-led service' has helped to push patients online for health advice and products. Fox et al. found

> Motivations to use the Internet for pharmaceutical acquisition include privacy, an unwillingness to pass through a professional gatekeeper, cost and purposes for which drugs are to be used ... [and] that motivations can best be understood in terms of orientation towards professional expertise, and that users of pharmaceuticals range along a continuum from those accepting medical expertise to those acting as autonomous consumers (Fox et al. 2005a, n.p.)

In some cases this has had a detrimental effect in the sense that it tends to deter individuals from interaction with healthcare professionals. Some lack trust in the NHS and begin to research, self-diagnose and self-prescribe online in the belief that professional gatekeepers and governmental structures are only concerned with cutting costs and not offering appropriate individual care. This was particularly apparent during the online ethnography in the context of mental health, as the following blog entry explains:

> Eight weeks ago, I decided to treat myself for bipolar, and went to a website to get the medication Lamotrigine. I stepped up the dosage slowly, as recommended by any number of helpful websites ... Why did I do this? Late in 2009 I had a bipolar episode ... Since then I've had three years of severe depression, with engagement in the NHS going from awful, to negligent, to life-threatening ... Specialists losing their jobs to cuts. Two wrong diagnoses. Cancelled appointments due to staff unavailability. Phone calls not returned. GPs with no clue about mental health issues ... 70 % of my prescriptions rejected at pharmacies because of GP errors, and having to go back and have them reissued because most GPs don't understand how to prescribe controlled substances properly ... About six months after the episode I'd researched all the medication options, and found one I'd thought was suitable ... My experience is common. I just wish I'd done this sooner ... The NHS mental health system is not fit for purpose

This autonomous consumer, having experienced negative encounters with the NHS, has been ideologically pushed towards a (neo)liberal vision of healthcare, moving from the negative experience of being an NHS patient to what is imagined to be a potentially positive alternative experience of being a sovereign consumer-citizen, independent and capable of choice and self-governance. The Internet therefore acts as the avenue through which this self-governance can take shape and become culturally affirmed by others. It offers information on health and illness, the medicinal products required and sites where it is possible to discuss experiences with others. Therefore, this can also be analysed in light of the literature on prosumption and communicative capitalism (Dean 2005), as an example of self-diagnosing and buying online, where lack of trust, anonymity and individualism combine as negative and positive, or 'push and pull', motivating factors. However, this consumer/patient is putting himself or herself at greater risk of harm; direct harms associated with the damaging health effects of consuming illicit medicines and indirect harms that can emerge as a result of self-managing their healthcare regime without the advice of a trained professional.

Considering recent reports that the mental health system in the UK is in crisis, with a nine per cent reduction in beds available to mental health patients reported over a 21-month period and a leading psychiatrist stating the system is 'inefficient' and 'unsafe' (Guardian Online 2013), the future prospect of increased numbers of mental health patients following a similar path of individualised healthcare is probable. This presents opportunities for counterfeiters to supply psychiatric medicines to UK consumers. We found mental health patients to be an especially at-risk group of consumers seeking illicit medicines. Along with cases such as the one above, our data suggest the existence of many users seeking medicine for depression and anxiety who do not want any evidence of these illnesses on their medical records. This includes those suffering from eating disorders, a field in which appetite suppressants are widely available, at risk of counterfeiting and widely used and promoted among users of pro-anorexia forums (see Sugiura et al. 2012).

Neoliberalism's political rhetoric of privatisation attempts to promote this as greater freedom, choice and input, and when supported by a culture of hyper-individualism, anxiety and suspicion and an NHS encouraging a new cultural norm of 'informed patients', interacts to erode faith in public services. Subsequently, more people take on a self-governing role in their healthcare, a culture that the Internet enables, reproduces and exploits. The following entry in a UK forum emphasises the impact the issue of sufficient physician–patient contact can have on the individual's decision to bypass healthcare regulations and use the Internet for pharmaceutical supplies:

> After trying to get a doctor's appointment for several weeks with no luck, I gave up and decided to go online to buy the drug I wanted – oxytetracy-cline which is supposed to be only available in the UK via a prescription … Now with more cutbacks to GP opening hours and people doing their own research on the net, it's now apparently quite common for people to do this. The fact that I'm saving money is not the reason I did this … it is because I've been trying for weeks to get a doctor's appointment but couldn't, so I went online did some research, then tried to get the treatment myself and its worked! The point I'm making is, more and more people are now doing this for the reasons stated, and this practice of ordering your chosen drug online is now quite common place, and will only continue to become more popular while the government carry on underfunding local GP practices and services

This is an example of a consumer/patient who would prefer a return to a more patient-centred NHS where further time is spent with professionals, who has moved to the Internet because he/she is unable to get the care they want from their local GP. This particular example conflicts with Fox et al.'s (2005b) analysis of the 'informed patient' feeling empowered and the notion that the cultural shift towards self-managing healthcare democ-ratises health experiences. Fox et al. do mention a 'double-edged sword', where on the one hand the Internet offers support and information about healthcare, yet on the other can promote mainstream and generalised con-structions of 'health and body shape'. For example, to be a certain body shape is to be healthy and medical solutions are available if the individual cannot achieve this condition by diet, exercise and so on (see Fox et al. 2005b: 1306). However, we have found consumer/patients who use the Internet for their pharmaceutical needs who are not only being left open to greater risks associated with illicit medicines, but who desire more face-to-face interaction with healthcare specialists. Sillence and Briggs (2007) found something similar during their qualitative research with UK con-sumers who use the Internet for health and fitness purposes:

> Time constraints in the consulting room have also led to an increase in online searching. The average length of an appointment with a family practi-tioner is currently about eight minutes. In this short period of time both the doctor and the patient find it difficult to explain and discuss all their issues.

Patients often think doctors do not give them enough information to make sensible choices about how they want to be treated and they often find it difficult to recall the specifics of their discussions with the doctor after the consultation. (2007: 2)

Thus a decrease in time available in surgeries with doctors is driving patients online, from which we can assume that, as the NHS continues to privatise and cut back on patient–doctor hours, the number of people seeking health advice and POMs online without prescription will increase.

Our research found that the growing privatisation of the NHS and an ideological thrust towards personal social responsibility has had a profoundly damaging effect on some health behaviours and the pharmaceutical trade. Principally, the private relationship between consumer and producer has begun to erode trust in public services, creating suspicion, as well as producing cutbacks in terms of care, as two further examples from the ethnography also highlight:

For most drugs there is unnecessary regulation surrounding their sale in the UK. It's more about keeping the GP's in the financial loop than patient safety.

There are government initiatives to scare people away from buying this stuff on the Internet. But as a previous poster said, once you find a reputable supplier then you are good. And there is no going back to the dark ages, when a couple such as my friend would be condemned to a sexless marriage in their late 40s.

As monetary exchange dominates, and direct interaction rarely takes place, individuals become more suspicious of legitimate healthcare structures. Indeed, the NHS can save money from this sort of 'DIY healthcare'. As the consumer/patient becomes more involved in the whole process of diagnoses, from researching their illness and diagnosing and prescribing online without face-to-face contact, fewer personnel hours are required.

Individual motivations and pre-existing attitudes impact not only on the decision to use the Internet, but also on the selection of the particular sites which can and should be used for health advice and products. As Sillence and Briggs (2007) found in a psychological study assessing the role of the Internet in health behaviour:

> Despite the ongoing concerns regarding quality of online information our studies and others … have shown that it is the users of Internet information rather than authors or professional experts who decide what and how material is accessed and used. Ultimately decisions concerning the selection of online material, and evaluations of its trustworthiness and quality will always be influenced by peoples' own particular motivations and cognitive biases. Online information highlights the struggle over expertise in the health domain. How the Internet affects health behaviour depends in part on the existing nature of the patient physician relationship and in part on the patients existing attitude towards his or her health. (Silence and Briggs 2007: 13)

We are not suggesting that the Internet cannot offer legitimate information on health and illness, or allow some patients better access, convenience and rewarding experiences. There is little doubt that legitimate and sensible healthcare and pharmaceutical consumption online can offer a number of benefits. However, in the context of illicit medicines and their supply and demand, it also offers numerous opportunities for criminal activity and personal or social harm, and the balance between these costs and benefits has yet to be adequately researched on a sufficiently large scale. The motivations behind those involved in the supply of illegitimate pharmaceuticals are obvious, and the Internet opens up opportunities to network and sell products online with less risk. Indeed, those accessing medicines online seem to have pre-existing attitudes and behaviours related to healthcare, prescription drugs and counterfeiting. The consumer rhetoric currently changing the NHS and the traditional patient–physician relationship is affecting health behaviours and, as we have seen in the cases above, fuelling the move to the Internet for healthcare. Overall, the rise of e-health and the commodification of healthcare (see Brijnath 2012), energised by increased desires from the new cultural norm of the consumer/patient, has helped to normalise online pharmaceutical consumption in the UK and opened up opportunities for the supply and demand of illicit medicines. Yet, beyond those self-diagnosing illness, the motivations behind the consumption and online purchase of pharmaceuticals are multifaceted, with some consumers more willing to risk the harm posed by illicit medicines for a variety of additional reasons.

Saving Face: The Demand for Lifestyle Medicines
Arguably, lifestyle medicines are drugs consumed through personal choice rather than illness, used for non-health matters or matters lying at the

margins of health and well-being (Flower 2004). This category includes cosmetic reasons, such as counteracting hair loss and accelerating weight loss, as well as medicines used to treat sexual dysfunction, for which we have found a large illicit market online in the UK. However, there is much debate surrounding the dichotomy often drawn between personal responsibility and healthcare (Gilbert et al. 2000), and the associated issue of the widespread medicalisation of non-medical issues. This is a contentious issue whose complexity is beyond the scope of this book, but, in brief, many commentators have criticised the medicalisation of sexual dysfunction and beauty. In the case of medicines used for cosmetic reasons, many emphasise a culture of lack and inadequacy based on an unattainable image of beauty, which is feeding the cosmetic industry's sales (see Fox et al. 2005c; Miah and Rich 2008). This culture, propagated by the mainstream marketing industry, has increased consumer demand but it has also been appropriated by illegitimate players—in some cases active criminals—who seek to move into this lucrative market. Forums and Web 2.0 can act to extend this cultural landscape; for example, Fox et al. (2005b) note that forums 'perpetuate a biomedical model of overweight as a condition to be overcome' (2005b, n.p.). Therefore, online social networking and discussion can also further increase feelings of lack and inadequacy already propagated by consumer culture, while simultaneously normalising pharmaceutical treatments and the medicalisation of these issues. In these forums users self-promote and network evaluative information about their perceived conditions and the experiences they have had with pharmaceuticals.

Online shopping offers a convenient and relatively anonymous way to stay in the comfort of the home and have goods delivered to the door. The convenience of an online diagnosis, purchase and delivery in the privacy of the home is especially significant as an influence on the demand for so-called lifestyle medicines. In this market the consumerist approach to health is most apparent (Fox and Ward 2006) and a privatised consumer experience is often sought. There is a huge global online market for lifestyle drugs, and some are arguably the most counterfeited products. The most in demand of this broad type of medicine are those offering a treatment for erectile dysfunction, weight loss or hair loss. In the UK, there is a growing trade in counterfeit Viagra and anabolic steroids (Yar 2008: 154). For obvious reasons there is a high demand for online purchase: consumers are too embarrassed to ask, or they want to use the drugs for something other than their intended purposes. For example, Viagra as a libido enhancer or appetite suppressants used by bodybuilders or young women suffering from anorexia nervosa.

Viagra and other drugs used to treat erectile dysfunction are now more readily available from supermarkets in the UK. However, for the basic reasons of saving embarrassment, avoiding stigma and searching for cheaper prices (see Cordell et al. 1996; Albers-Miller 1999), most people still prefer to order online. As the following comment thread highlights:

> My "friend" (really it's not me) buys generic Cialis regularly for £2 a pill (breaks it up and it lasts him a week). It's hard to overstate how this has changed his life (and that of his wife). They had basically given up on sex, it would hardly work; now they've had a great normal sex life for the last 5 years. No, he wouldn't be given access to the drug from a doctor as he has no underlying medical condition. So get real. There are government initiatives to scare people away from buying this stuff on the Internet. But as a previous poster said, once you find a reputable supplier then you are good. And there is no going back to the dark ages, when a couple such as my friend would be condemned to a sexless marriage in their late 40s.

As a result, most junk/spam folders include large numbers of emails offering cheap Viagra. Estimates suggest that '25 % of all email, approximately 15 billion messages per day, is spam advertising counterfeit and/or unlicensed, unapproved drugs' (see Jackson et al. 2012). Such is the mass of information on the Internet about Viagra that it can confuse consumers when they attempt to figure out which are fakes. We found an entire blog dedicated to 'good and cheap Viagra', where products are tested by consumers who leave feedback for others. Again, Web 2.0 facilitates this process of prosumption. Some websites use the competition between the better-known brands—Viagra, Tadalafil or Cialis—or comparisons between various active ingredients in medicines for erectile dysfunction to advertise consumer preferences. They also include standard incentives and marketing tactics to increase the volume of orders, such as discounts or free extras. Occasionally products to treat erectile dysfunction are offered as a free addition to orders for stimulants, opioids or steroids.

The market for anabolic steroids in the UK has in some respects moved online particularly for those consumers who are not embedded in the gym and bodybuilding scene and do not have access to suppliers offline (see also Antonopoulos and Hall 2016). This pattern is evident in a number of other countries (see Paoli and Donati 2014). These consumers, who are mostly 'occasional' steroid users, look primarily online for merchandise. There are numerous opportunities to buy products and visit a vast array of forums dedicated to shared experiences of diets, exercise regimes and pharmaceutical assistance. Again, forums and social networking play a pivotal role in the consumer experience. In gym and bodybuilding subcultures the demand for steroids and various appetite suppressants and supplements is high, and there is evidence suggesting a large *counterfeit* market in operation, especially in the context of the online trade. The most popular steroids Deca-Durabolin ('Deca', in trader and user vernacular), Winstrol ('Winny') and injectable testosterone are among the most counterfeited PIEDs. The problem is so acute that an e-book titled *The Secrets of Mail Order Steroid Success* was published in 2004 (Spellwin 2004). It provides advice to users ordering steroids online looking to minimise the possibility of buying and consuming counterfeit products and has become extremely popular among the frequenters of forums providing information about steroids.

Drug Diversion: Recreational Drug Use and Prescription Drug Misuse
The demand for online prescription drugs in the UK is also fuelled by the phenomenon of drug diversion for recreational motives and prescription drug misuse. While there are no clear divisions between the drugs available online, whether they are marketed or consumed for recreational, pharmaceutical or 'lifestyle' purposes (Walsh 2011: 57), the diversion of so many prescription drugs from their suggested use plays a significant role in the expansion of demand for online sales. Firstly, there is the obtainability and convenience of POMs without prescription, delivered directly to the consumer's home address. Secondly, drug forums in particular—although many advertise harm reduction—act to increase the user's knowledge of drugs, especially methods of use, combinations and effects. Again, social networking functions as both advertiser and marketer of specific drugs, often for unintended use, which can increase online demand and open up the further avenues for the supply of counterfeits.

Recreational Pharmaceutical Drug Use
Neilson and Barrat (2009) note that online drug forums assist the user in accessing information on how to use prescription medicines recreationally by providing

> ... specific knowledge about how to diverge from the medication's legal instructions to obtain the desired effects, which might include specific dosages, different administration routes, combinations, or obtaining one compound from a combination (2009: 5)

Examples from the ethnographic research include entire threads on drug forums dedicated to various deviatory experiences, from questions and answers on 'How to smoke Percocet', 'Gabapentin recreational use' and 'Can you get high off Trazodone?'. Some evaluate the negative and positive effects, discussing issues such as euphoria, sedation, anaesthesia and the nature of the subsequent 'come down'.

Other threads explain the process of various administrative techniques and effects as well as soliciting and circulating advice and experience from other users:

> So SWIM pops a 7.5 mg Zopiclone pill, waits for the effect, nothing happens, he goes home ... he takes out another pill, places it on foil and lights it from underneath, takes 2 hits, starts feeling the euphoria that comes with it and the relaxing feelings. So he takes 2 more hits and now he's high, bad balance (which is funny) euphoric and just sitting here relaxing after those 4 hits, the pill got all brown so then SWIM tried taking another hit, didn't work, so he crushed it up, poorly though, didn't work so SWIM has a few questions. Does it not work to smoke more if it's all brown? If you can, what should SWIM do? And should SWIM let the pill slide down and create this gooey stuff? Cause that didn't seem to work, maybe pills only do that when they're water soluble. When SWIM smokes on foil, Zopiclone pills, should he crush them up or smoke them like they are? If SWIM smokes a pill like it is, can he pop it afterwards?

Another user answers:

> SWIM is gonna try and smoke one right now and see if it can still be smoked when darkened and if it leaves a gooey trail.

These users are virtually communicating their new prescription drug experiences and the different combinations and administrative techniques associated with the recreational use of pharmaceutical products. The acronym SWIM—Someone Who Isn't Me—is used to avoid self-incrimination on these forums. Here, the dominance of libertine sentiments towards the recreational use of prescription drugs in forums normalises this form of drug taking and experimentation. Forum users often discuss buying POMs online, although discussing sites for supply is discouraged and public posts are taken down if the actual name of a supplier is mentioned.

We found many occasions where medicines were being used for something other than their intended purpose, whether for self-medication or hedonistic pleasure. Polydrug use was also evident, and many users recalled incidents when they had 'completely blacked out' or were 'totally wasted' or 'got totally off my head' after mixing Valium or Oxycodone with huge quantities of alcohol on a night out, or mixing stimulants and opioids for 'a buzz' or to induce hallucinations. Therefore, unintended methods, combinations and administration techniques contribute to the online demand for illicit medicines:

> SWIM started with 60 mg Adderall and let that kick in. Half an hour later, he added 10 mg Zolpidem and 30 mg Adderall. Within 20 minutes he felt this totally lucid, clear-minded euphoria he hasn't experienced on any legal drug. After an hour, he repeated with the 10/30 mg combo of the Zolpidem and Adderall. Whew ... at that point he was flying high and totally carefree. That was nearly 2 hours ago and SWIM is still in that mindset.SWIM can clearly recall everything he's done since the first pill he's taken tonight. He's spoken to friends online and via text message without coming off as odd at all. SWIM says that this is the favorite combo he may have found so far. It apparently takes a massive amount of stimulants (remember SWIM in total took 120 mg Adderall – twice the manufacturers recommended max dose – to offset just two 10 mg Zolpidem). Not only that, but SWIM isn't wired AT ALL. Sleep could come easy right now. It would take another 30 mg+ of amphetamine before he'd say he had an 'upper' combo from the two.

Numerous discussions can be found in drug forums regarding research chemicals, legal highs and illicit drugs that relate to prescription drug use. Whether they are discussing practices or suppliers, consumers seemed to appreciate the opportunities this presented for them to share their experiences. These consumers were moving their drug practices online, sometimes to bypass legitimate supply chains. They were particularly at risk of consuming illicit medicines, yet also more likely to knowingly buy and risk the harm of these medicines bought online. Therefore, there is a huge crossover between the demand for illicit medicines and drug misuse and recreational use, with forums playing an important role in sharing information on new chemicals and cocktails.

Moreover, because the growth of the night-time economy in the UK has led to higher levels of recreational drug use, particularly with regard to stimulants, amphetamines and new synthetic party drugs, there is evidence that prescription medicines are not only bought online as an alternative high, but to counteract the deleterious after-effects of using illicit drugs. We gathered evidence of a number of online prescription drugs used to counteract the effects of illicit drugs. One offline respondent orders non-benzodiazepines such as Zopiclone as a countermeasure for her cocaine use. Similarly, a forum thread from the online ethnography highlights something similar with regard to Valium and ecstasy:

> Always have a few vallies or similar in stock to kill the sleep paralysis that hits a couple of nights after [ecstasy] pills

Aware of this link, and of the general outlook that buying POMs online to consume recreationally can be less risky than buying illicit drugs on the street, the producers and distributors of new synthetic drugs also produce and distribute pharmaceutical drugs (see Chap. 4). As Neilson and Barratt (2009) point out, dealers use the Internet for drug acquisition and consumers gather information about using prescription drugs recreationally and having them delivered to their home. Therefore, in the context of the online trade in illicit medicines, there is a significant mutually reinforcing crossover between demand for legal highs and illicit drugs in terms of both production and consumption.

We also found cases of stimulants such as Ritalin, which is officially prescribed to treat attention deficit hyperactivity disorder, being diverted and taken to aid concentration and memory. In terms of social harm this is a worrying development. As Walsh (2011) points out:

> probably the most dangerous aspect of this trade is the understandable yet insidious assumption— the result of a lifetime's indoctrination with false distinctions—that prescription drugs (even when purchased off-prescription) are inherently safer than street drugs. The risk for overdose and dependence derives from the dosage, potency of the drug and the vulnerability of the person using it—not the source of the drug or its brand name. (2011: 57)

This leads to another factor found by our initial research to be fuelling consumer demand for online medicines. It seems that certain UK consumers who operate on the online sites that are the regular avenues for illicit medicine supply were particularly vulnerable to prescription drug misuse.

Prescription Drug Misuse

During the course of the virtual ethnography, many forum discussions and posts revealed that consumers are buying medicines via the Internet to feed a prescription drug habit, sometimes in order to 'top up' their prescriptions, because they have either grown tolerant to their prescribed amount and require more or they have reached the limit on the amount of scripts a healthcare professional will prescribe. Rutter and Bryce (2008) also found this to be a key motivation for the consumption of counterfeit products more generally, where 'the use of counterfeit goods was part of a strategy through which to manage their whole range of consumption' and 'as a means of allowing them to increase the number of items they could afford' (2008: 1157). Here motivation expands beyond price to the consumers' desire to increase the volume of a medicine their physician prescribes, which has been restricted usually because of a high potential of misuse.

The misuse of prescription drugs is on the rise (Nielson and Barrat 2009). The most commonly abused are opioids, stimulants and central nervous system (CNS) depressants or sedatives. The virtual ethnography highlighted many instances of prescription drug misuse, where consumers have turned to online methods for the drugs' sheer availability. However, in some cases online consumption is only one avenue used in order to buy large quantities of prescription-only drugs and can act as a force multiplying their addictive tendencies:

> I know someone else who's buying Valium ... online and she's now become addicted to them.
>
> I've been taking them [Zopiclone] for years on and off, initially from my doctor ... she had me on them for about 6 months, unknown to me was how addictive they were ... a year on and I went weeks without a wink of sleep, I knew Zopiclone could help, so I found an Internet site I could get them from as my doctor would not prescribe me Zopiclone again ... anyway as I had some knowledge of Zopiclone from before, still not fully understanding the extent to which I would become dependent on them, I started taking them ... this turned into a habit where I have reached the point ... I am taking about 8–10 7.5 mg tablets a day just to feel normal.

In the second case medical exposure led to misuse of non-benzodiazepines, a drug whose misuse potential is notably high. Analgesics were also in high demand from drug misusers. One UK-based study found that 76 per cent of the online pharmacies in their sample sold prescription analgesics without prescriptions (Raine et al. 2008: 253). Our interviews with health professionals also revealed that on some occasions individuals attempting to obtain POMs online is the side effect or the unintended consequence of successful law enforcement against a physical/offline market in illegal drugs. The following case is indicative: In late 2012, the police in a town in the North of England decided to have a heavier presence on the streets of a particular ward/neighbourhood which presented a significant drug-use rate and observable, street-level illegal drug supply that were associated with heightened levels of public disorder. In the process, and with the assistance of intelligence officers, the police managed to take out a number of key players in the business, players who were personally connected with central 'actors' from groups of teenagers and young adults associated with 'sessions' in the particular locale. These 'sessions' were events in specific public and private venues dedicated to drug taking and alcohol consumption. In light of law enforcement success and the gap that this created in the drugs market (see Hoffer et al. 2009), the youngsters started organising 'sessions' in private venues with pharmaceutical drugs, including POMs that were either stolen from their parents and grandparents cupboards or were ordered online.

These consumer practices pose significant health risks. As Holloway et al. (2013) highlight, '[i]n 2010, 14 % of drug-related death certificates issued in England and Wales mentioned anti-depressants, 11 % reported consumption of benzodiazepines and 2 % mentioned Zopiclone' (2013: 1). Therefore, online supply chains are putting consumers at greater risk of the dangers of overdosing as well as ingesting illicit medicines, which can increase dependence and in some cases lead to death. The following excerpt highlights the facilitating impact Internet supply had on one individual user's prescription drug misuse:

> I had decided to Google the drug to see if I could buy it online, and to my surprise, without much effort at all I found a supplier, he was based in the UK and so I began placing orders, receiving it the next day via Royal Mail Recorded Delivery .... This was soooo much easier than using the GP but as you will discover this was probably the biggest mistake I ever made in my life ... I began by ordering 10 tablets – I was not sure if it was all a scam and did not want to put serious money in, just a few pound. I made a few other smaller orders and all were straight forward, easy and I always got my pills the next day. Due to this I started buying in bulk – 100 pills at a time ... This abundance however proved to be an issue, I soon found myself taking two tablets a night, then three, then four .... This 100 tablets did not last me 100 nights at all ... I then found another supplier, they were overseas but the price was tiny. I started ordering 200 at a time, the same cycle of taking five, six, seven each night began to happen ... I had spiralled into dependency, tolerance and addiction. I had become a drug addict without knowing it, of course now I know they are addictive but when I first started

taking them I had no idea the extent to which I would be effected by this powerful sedative hypnotic drug

Furthermore, it is well documented that in the US addiction to prescription opioids and opioid misuse has grown to epidemic proportions and is a leading cause of drug deaths. This is now becoming a problem in the UK as consumers have more opportunities to buy large quantities of POMs via the Internet.

Anti-Big Business Sentiment? Attitudes Towards Counterfeiting
One other factor to consider is consumer attitudes towards counterfeiting. Drawing on the UK research, Chaudry and Zimmerman argue that the main factors behind the consumer demand for illicit goods online include 'consumer complicity', anti-big business sentiment, a lack of concern for intellectual property rights (IPR) and a common belief that fakes can offer the quality of the trademarked item (2009: 21). We found some of these sentiments among consumers during the virtual ethnography:

> It is thoroughly absurd that perfectly good generic or branded medications should be available online sometimes for as little as a tenth of the cost of getting them through approved means. From what I'm reading the ... attempts to curtail sales from entirely respectable Canadian online pharmacies seems to have more to do with protecting profits rather than people. Yes, I've ordered on-line and yes, I would do so again if I thought there was a need.

Ironically, this individual is unaware that the 'Canadian Pharmacy' brand name is run by a large criminal organisation whose main aim is also to profit from consumer/patients, but without any regulatory oversight. Furthermore, as Edwards et al. (2012) point out in their study of music and film downloads, the emergence of digital technologies has invoked in the consumer a further demand for 'free and unfettered access' to copyrighted materials. However, there is a significant difference in the products being traded and the harm their consumption causes. For example, luxury fashion and entertainment goods must be seen as distinct from safety-critical goods, in terms of their potential social harm and their regulation and policing. As Wall and Large's (2010) research suggests, there is little public will for the policing of luxury goods markets, thus this trade should be 'separated out' from safety-critical goods such as medicines and seen in a separate domain of regulation and control.

There are also broad-ranging public attitudes towards intellectual property and willingness to buy counterfeits. This is particularly interesting when we consider the context of deceptive and non-deceptive counterfeits. A relatively recent EU survey highlighted that five per cent of consumers thought they may have received counterfeit medicine in ways that involve deception by the seller (Jackson et al. 2012). However, there are others who intentionally buy illicit medicinal products to save money, and have little concern about intellectual property crime. Other consumers actively dislike IPR and big business, as this forum entry highlights:

> I've previously bought drugs online without prescription from very reliable pharmacy sites. Just like when I've been abroad and bought drugs directly over the counter that would require a prescription here in the UK. For most drugs there is unnecessary regulation surrounding their sale in the UK. It's more about keeping the GP's in the financial loop than patient safety.

Podder et al. (2011) argue that differences in attitudes and practices amongst consumers are 'dependent on moral beliefs', whereas Swami et al. (2009) have argued that they are dependent on individual differences and personality traits. Indeed these factors will have a substantial effect on buying behaviour and attitudes towards counterfeit products. However, this also varies depending on the nature of the product, with differences in opinion regarding safety-critical goods.

Data collected for this study did include some animosity felt towards patents, IPR price increases and the 'criminogenic' mainstream pharmaceutical industry more broadly (see Ehrenreich et al. 1980; Braithwaite 1984; Wohl 1984; Fisse and Braithwaite 1993; Passas 2005; Singh Bansal et al. 2009; Goldacre 2012) seen as inadequately controlled in the way they do business (see Moynihan et al. 2002; Law 2006; Cernea and Uszkai 2012). As a discussant in a forum we examined suggested:

> God knows what they [pharmaceutical companies] feed us with and what they inject us with. And, of course, with a doctor's prescription ... with a small detail ... the doctor sees the content of the medicine from the label and he will never do a personal chemical analysis of the medicine ... Even if it contains what it says on the label, no doctor is going to examine what's in ... In other words, a small number of scientists – who work for multinational pharmaceutical companies – will do this for us, before us Generally, very few know the truth about the scientific data and the rest just accept them on credit ... If your doctor prescribed it to you, should you just not worry?

However, consumer attitudes did not seem to be strong enough to sug-gest that anti-big business sentiment is a key determinant factor. Rather, our research supports the findings of Rutter and Bryce (2008). According to their survey results, the UK consumers of counterfeit products gener-ally do not show anti-big business sentiment. Instead, their counterfeit consumption practices were used as a way 'to increase consumption of lei-sure goods' to meet their needs and desires 'rather than to undermine the market' (2008: 1157). Therefore, instead of analysing the UK consumers' consumption of illicit medicines on the premise that attitudes are the prod-uct of countercultural efforts to undermine the mainstream pharmaceutical industry or governments, or by pure economic rationality (i.e. determined by price), so far we have found that the consumption of illicit medicines is 'a widespread, situated and everyday practice' (ibid.). Indeed, many respondents spoke about the increased prices they found online. We should also be aware that often consumers may be completely unaware they are consuming fakes in the first instance, or, for reasons outlined above, may be more willing to risk the harm associated with fakes, as we found with the example of recreational users and misusers of prescription drugs.

Whether the consumer lacks trust in the NHS, is too embarrassed to seek help, cannot get an appointment with a healthcare professional, or whether they are feeding a prescription drug habit for which healthcare professionals are unwilling to issue a prescription, the virtual ethnography found that various permutations of these factors are the principal con-tributors to the rise of the online consumption of illicit medicines in the UK. Depending on the specific pharmaceutical product and intended use this left particular demographic groups at more risk of social harm and/or more willing to take part in deviant behaviour.

Who Is at Risk? Measuring Demographic Variables

It is difficult to unpack demographic variables via a virtual ethnography, for obvious reasons such as the anonymity, hidden identities and pseud-onyms on virtual sites. However, bearing in mind the contributing factors examined above and the specific medicines most regularly bought online, according to data generated in the virtual ethnography, offline ethnog-raphy and the review of secondary sources it seems a range of demo-graphic groups in the UK are more likely to buy medicine online and therefore more at risk of consuming illicit pharmaceuticals and suffering harms. However, important common factors intersect this range of social groups. Littlejohn et al. (2005) propose three 'prerequisites' a consumer must have to be able to purchase pharmaceuticals online: literacy, Internet access and credit card ownership.

There are high rates of literacy in the UK and the 'number of people in Britain who are using the Internet has risen substantially, reaching 78 % of the population aged 14 years and over as compared with 59 % in 2003' (Blank 2013). However, in terms of credit card ownership, our research found instances online where the offer of directly paying money into a supplier's bank account, or via MoneyGram, PayPal or Western Union, was available as a payment option; therefore, credit card ownership was not always a necessity. Rutter and Bryce found consumption of counterfeits happens 'across the entire range of age, gender and socioeconomic status' (2008: 1158), a finding which our virtual ethnography supports. However, there are obvious demographic differences when we compare specific pharmaceuticals and their intended purposes. If we consider Viagra for instance, this product will be almost entirely consumed by men, infertility treatments will be consumed by women in certain age groups struggling to conceive, or as the case with Clomid, also men involved in bodybuilding. However, the virtual ethnography has revealed some further complexities that require analysis.

Socioeconomic Factors

In US research on consumer demand and susceptibility, analyses usually focus on the 'sickest' and the 'poorest' as the main demographic group, and price as the key determinant factor (see Ivanitskaya et al. 2010). However, the UK context seems to be more complex. POMs often cost more when sold without prescription online, therefore for this reason alone saving money (price) is not a key determinant factor. This highlights other cultural and demographic factors at play: the need/desire for the product without prescription; the tendency for higher socioeconomic groups to shop for these products online and the UK consumer regarded as a prime target by online sellers because of the higher returns on offer. UK consumers tend to have a larger amount of disposable income. This was examined by Littejohn et al. (2005) during their study of Internet pharmacies and consumers in Scotland. They found that individuals seeking pharmaceuticals online tended to come from social groups with higher levels of education and employment, including those we can regard as 'expert-patients' who may have more confidence to self-diagnose online.

Other secondary sources also point to the fact that in the UK online drug prices are not necessarily cheaper (see Raine et al. 2008) and are in fact sometimes more expensive. Therefore, the principal factors seem to be the availability of online medicines and the culturally specific desires/needs of the consumers. During the online ethnography we found this to be the case for one user who was 'stocking up' to pre-empt illness:

My main reason is that I am a bit of a survivalist and I'd like to stock certain types of medications for that worst-case scenario, including antibiotics, injections of morphine, iodine, etc. These are all things that if you walk into your doctor's office and say you'd like a prescription for, he's going to laugh you out of the office. So I've been trying to find a way I can buy some of this stuff to keep in my emergency kit. The real trouble is that most of it will expire in a year or two and I'll have to replace it. So I need a reliable way of buying it every few years. I've been afraid to give my money to these online pharmacies because I'm afraid they'll ship me fake medicine or nothing at all. Any advice?

An offline respondent also displayed this particular behaviour. A wealthy individual in the UK we interviewed also 'stocks up' on a variety of prescription medicines online, including benzodiazepines to counteract his illicit cocaine use, Viagra, anti-histamines, anabolic steroids and antibiotics. He is aware of the risk of interception, but because money is not a prohibitive issue he buys often and in bulk. These are examples of privatised and hyper-individual health/drug practices, where price is not considered important in the practices of purchase and consumption.

However, this does not mean it is only the rich who can access or buy illicit medicines online. Two socioeconomic issues are important to consider. On the one hand, access to credit has become easier and, on the other, access to technology is simpler. As Littlewood et al.'s study also contended, 'efforts to bridge the digital divide may increase access to Internet-sourced drugs amongst those in lower socioeconomic groups' (2005: 75), which, with the growing availability of credit and increasingly free Internet access, has opened up opportunities for those from less privileged backgrounds to risk consuming illicit medicines bought online. In the online market for smaller quantities of POMs, particularly via social networking sites, we found a broad range of socioeconomic groups.

Young People and Teenagers

Young people are particularly at risk because they are close to the age of onset of many drugs of abuse (Holloway et al. 2013). Moreover, they are very active online, particularly on social networking sites. Drug use precipitated by the pressures of academic performance is common (ibid.). For the basic reason that these drugs are so readily available via the Internet, young people in the UK are more susceptible to buying and consuming them. The move online to user-generated content and participatory web cultures has opened up opportunities for young people to access information and share experiences about pharmaceutical consumption. As we touched on earlier, Facebook, forums and blogs culturally normalise recreational prescription drug use, misuse and experimentation.

Young people in particular are turning to the Internet rather than to a family doctor or a parent for health information and advice, and the appeal of the Internet is particularly strong for those people who seek advice on important but sensitive matters (Klein and Wilson 2003). The number of hours spent by young people on the Internet has now surpassed TV, and with the affordability and accessibility of digital technologies—from tablets to mobile phones—online drugs are more easily attainable to this demographic group in the UK. Furthermore, online trade increases accessibility and decreases the fears and risks associated with meeting a drug dealer in person. One relatively recent study examined university students in Wales and found that they were particularly perceptible to consuming pain relievers, tranquillisers and sedatives. The main motives for misuse were to obtain the therapeutic benefits of the drug, recreational purposes and mood enhancement (Holloway et al. 2013).

From reviewing the literature and conversations online, it seems that young people and teenagers are significantly at risk of consuming illicit medicines, and the determinant factors seem to overlap with drug diversion, whether for recreational drug use or drug misuse. Sometimes experimentation—seeking information online and then buying—combined with the inability to buy illicit drugs offline pushes young people towards the Internet in order to purchase a pharmaceutical equivalent. Also some young school or university students purchase POMs during exam periods for attention improvement (see, e.g. Foxton's 2012 example of an online drug dealer seeing a gap in this market; also Holloway's 2013 evidence relating to the UK students prescription drug consumption). This overlaps with the issues of price and disregard for purity as young people seek out the cheaper option and are more willing to risk harm as they consume illicit medicines.

Gender

Although men have begun to invest more resources in beauty and 'body maintenance', women on average still spend more time on these activities. There is no space here to explore the gendered cultural reasons behind this, but needless to say, this arguably places women at greater risk of consuming illicit medicines designed for lifestyle purposes relating to body weight and cosmetics. However, in the specific cases of the 'bodybuilding industry', the market in erectile dysfunction drugs and hair-loss medications, this gender balance shifts to men (see McDonald and Wearing 2013: 39).

We found women at risk of consuming fake fertility drugs, usually turning online to search for a cheaper option—in these cases price was a key determinant factor. These general patterns were confirmed in the virtual ethnography; it was predominantly females in forums for weight loss, therefore, for these medicines, women are more likely to be at risk, whereas men were more likely to buy anabolic steroids and drugs for erectile dysfunction.

There is some evidence to suggest that women are more likely to use medicines for non-medical purposes. One study 'states that "illicit use" of prescription drugs is an "alarming pattern among females" and cites figures for 2005–2010, which show that across 14 European countries, 13 per cent of women had tried tranquilizers or sedatives at some stage in their life-courses, compared with 7.9 per cent of men' (Beckford 2012). Moreover, Sillence and Briggs (2007) found that females are more likely to search for health matters online, reporting 76 per cent of a sample of 1900 respondents going online for health matters were female. However, we could gather no conclusive evidence that prescription drug diversion was gender-specific. Our research found that, overall, the increase in demand for medicines online is not gender specific and that the groups at risk depend more on the specific drug and the intended purpose.

Conclusion

Globalisation and the Internet has changed the social organisation and expanded the opportunities in the field of pharmaceutical consumption. The specific case of demand for illicit pharmaceuticals in the UK is a particularly complex one. The demand for illicit medicines has in some ways been initiated and extended by the expansion of ICT and specific political and economic structures and cultural transformations, which have prevented the implementation of effective regulatory action and legal deterrents for criminals operating in this field. Consumer demand in the UK is not an example of criminal behaviour but of deviancy. There are no legal sanctions in place in the UK for importing POMs via the Internet for personal use.

In the case of healthcare and pharmaceutical consumption, the Internet has significantly changed economic and sociocultural practices. Web 2.0 and participatory online networks have played an active role in normalising online health practices and pharmaceutical consumption, and also perform a crucial marketing and advertising function. Moreover, online pharmaceutical consumption has also been further intensified by the global diffusion of free-market processes and ideology. The current discourse of consumerism and practices of public-sector reform in the UK have increased the demand for pharmaceuticals online, which has in turn opened up and expanded the opportunities for the trade in illicit medicines over the Internet, putting the consumer/patient at risk of physical and psychological harm. A range of factors contribute to the demand and a range of demographic groups are at risk of consuming illicit medicines, which include consumer/patients taking a more active role in their own healthcare and moving online for all manner of health-related information and products. Overall, these consumption patterns are situated everyday practices. Therefore, the trade in illicit medicines online is a specific example of the dialectical relationship between online and offline 'worlds', each seeking out immanent problems in each other's practices and achieving synthetic solutions that match supply with a suite of increasingly complex and persistent consumer desires. Consumers and sellers never physically meet, yet a physical product can be produced, distributed and administered with little regulation and increased risks of causing physical harm to consumers. This chapter has shown that the demand for illicit medicines online should be analysed in the intersecting contexts of shifting late-modern consumption norms and practices, including those of drug use, the privatisation of public services and emergent technologies of pharmaceutical production, marketing and distribution.

CHAPTER 4

The Supply Side

Abstract This chapter focuses on the supply side, examining the dynamics shaping the physical flows of illicit medicines around the world. First, it explores the political economy of supply, which exposes the use of historically established trade routes, Special Economic Zones (SEZs) and parallel trading practices in the illicit pharmaceutical supply chain. Second, it offers a zonal model that outlines the most regularly utilised channels and routes through which illicit medicines are produced and distributed. Third, the chapter explores the social organisation of the illicit medicine trade. The data from investigative case files are presented and, along with other sources, highlight the key actors involved in the trade in the UK, their motivations, how they are organised and how the trade can be conceptualised as a by-product of the legal industry.

Keywords supply • special economic zones • parallel trade • organised crime • pharmaceutical industry

It has been argued that in the context of the online trade in illicit medicines too much emphasis is placed on cybercriminals and online trading companies at the expense of appreciating how the trade functions in the 'real' world (Guarnieri and Przyswa 2013). Indeed, the trade requires organisation, investment and the maintenance of a complex

© The Author(s) 2016
A. Hall, G.A. Antonopoulos, *Fake Meds Online*,
DOI 10.1057/978-1-137-57088-8_4

supply chain in material products. Drawing on our primary and secondary data, this chapter offers a detailed picture of the supply side of the illicit medicine trade, paying particular attention to the physical flows of illicit medicines around the globe. It will develop an understanding of how the trade functions, the actors involved and the principal avenues through which illicit medicines are manufactured and distributed. Accordingly, the chapter provides initial answers to the following research questions:

- What are the dynamics shaping the supply of illicit medicines in the UK and globally?
- How is the trade in illicit medicines embedded in the broader processes and structures of the global political economy?
- What are the channels, networks and spaces of production, transit and distribution?
- Who are the main actors involved in the trade and how are they organised?

Supplementing our argument regarding the trade's embeddedness in the late-capitalist global political economy and the blurred boundaries between legality and illegality, the chapter begins by discussing a set of politico-economic processes and structures through which the world has witnessed a growth in illicit medicine supply. This will include issues relating to trade routes, parallel trading practices and the use of Special Economic Zones (SEZs). A discussion of the offline physical flows of illicit medicines follows, which explores zones of production, transit and distribution. Finally, the trade's social organisation is explored in order to outline the actors (both illegal and legal) involved in the trade, how they are organised and how they are connected to one another. For this we use data collected from the online and offline ethnographies, as well as investigative case files, some of which will be presented as illustrative boxes in the chapter.

The Political Economy of Supply

Throughout our research, we have found that a number of specific late-capitalist international trade relations and practices, accompanied by the liberalisation of markets globally, have been principal determining factors that have helped expand the illicit medicine trade.

Historically Established Trade Routes

The emergence of globalisation and the market economy in Central and Eastern Europe after the collapse of the Soviet Union increased the number of illicit economies. Business people in the region began investing in illegal activities and the Balkans became a busy transit zone for illicit goods and services shipped from manufacturers situated in South and East Asia and the Middle East; usually headed to 'richer' consumer economies in Western Europe and the USA (see Portes et al. 1991). We have found evidence of this in cases relating to illicit medicines. Our evidence also suggests that Russia has become one of the largest producers of illicit medicines and West Africa a central geographic area for the distribution of illicit goods, a position achieved by developing illicit drug routes through Latin America and taking advantage of the increased availability of illicit medicines produced in China.

As Ellis (2009) argues, the neoliberal structural adjustment (SA) period in the 1980s, along with widespread corruption amongst heads of state implicated in the trafficking of drugs, destabilised legitimate economies in some West African states. Various smuggling routes that had emerged in the trade of cocaine and heroin in the 1950s facilitated intensified activity. Working from bases in countries such as Liberia, with its ideal transport facilities by sea and air and use of the dollar, West African traffickers became integral to the global transit and trafficking of illicit goods, establishing themselves as a vital node in the arterial distribution process. West African diasporic communities also situated themselves in useful locations around the globe, clearly positioned to continue business relations with drug producers. For example, traffickers operating in the large Nigerian community in Mumbai took advantage of India's position as a global leader in pharmaceutical production, and similar operations were set up in various parts of South Africa. Another crucial causal factor has been the nature and dynamics of Nigerian and other West African 'organised crime' syndicates. The social composition of their business model is notably flexible, or what is now often labelled an "adhocracy", far more suited to the modern day business environment than the traditional hierarchical structure (see Ellis 2009: 185). For these reasons we can identify an important West African connection in both the illicit pharmaceutical and narcotics trades.

The illicit medicine trade offers a profitable low-risk opportunity (see IRACM 2013: 18), which is why many formerly involved in relatively high-risk narco-trafficking have recently moved into the trade (see also Bate 2008). The African connection in the illicit pharmaceutical trade is confirmed by data we collected from law enforcement agencies (LEAs), the in-house anti-counterfeiting team of a large pharmaceutical company, and in discussions with African pharmaceutical company workers based in the UK, who specifically identified a South African connection in relation to production processes (see also Angop 2013).

The developing connection between Africa and China is also an important factor. As Ellis notes, 'with the recent emergence of China as a major diplomatic and business operator in Africa', alongside the history of Chinese criminals situated on the continent, collaborative developments in 'new illicit markets in China' have emerged (Ellis 2009: 196). One of the primary examples is the illicit pharmaceutical trade. The Chinese–Angolan connection is a particularly interesting point to consider. Data on seizures that we collected from a pharmaceutical company suggest that a direct trade route in illicit medicines from China through Angola to Europe and beyond is now in full operation. This new illicit trade route is the product of a relationship originally forged via legitimate political and economic arrangements that began to take shape when resource rich Angola, struggling to pay debts built up during the war for independence, was offered an oil-backed loan by China at a better rate than the IMF (see also Ford 2013). Now trade relations between the nations have intensified and a Chinese diaspora in various Southern, Eastern and West African countries is well positioned to nurture business relations in both legal and illegal markets. As Haugen notes '[t]he pace of growth in the commercial relations between China and African countries in the past decade has been remarkably high. Trade between China and Africa grew by an average of 28 per cent per annum between 1999 and 2009 in terms of monetary value adjusted for inflation' (Haugen 2011: 160).

Latin America's relationship with West Africa, forged in the trade of cocaine to Europe, has also been effective in presenting opportunities for the illicit medicine trade. One example is that of Guinea-Bissau's involvement in the illicit cocaine trade from Latin America to Europe (see UNODC 2007). Latin America is second only to Asia as a region where a large number of 'incidents' of counterfeit medicines have been reported (IRACM 2013: 17). Our data from a pharmaceutical company verify that claim. One notable example is a set of trade routes to Africa that have developed out of Colombia, where manufacturers producing large quantities of illicit medicines and packaging have exploited the routes already established via the traditional cocaine trade to distribute their products.

The Use of Special Economic Zones

Another crucial politico-economic process facilitating the illicit medicine trade is the establishment of so-called SEZs, which include free ports, free trade zones and export processing zones. From the manufacturing of huge swathes of commodities in an export development zone such as that situated in Chittagong in Bangladesh, to the transiting of products through free ports and free zones located in Nigeria, the United Arab Emirates (UAE) and Indonesia, these designated geographical zones are regularly used to transit illicit medicines. As deregulated conduits, free zones offer the unrestricted movement of commodities in spaces with the least resistance in terms of tax, policing, and health and safety. They are the perfect illustration of the logic of late capitalism, in as much as they are designed to offer loosened economic laws, sitting 'outside' the standard regulatory structure and, therefore, exempt from the nation state's laws that govern their physical geographical location. For example, they guarantee business-friendly economic environmental factors such as the free flow of capital, lower taxes on imports and exports, and working conditions with no minimum wage or working hours, all of which support profit maximisation, attract inward foreign investment and guarantee less risk in terms of policing. The rise of BRIC countries (Brazil, Russia, India, China) as the production hubs of the world (see EFPIA 2012), historically established criminal distribution channels and networks, and the formation of global SEZs combine to play an important role in the supply of illicit medicines and can be analysed as part of a general process of global capitalist zoning (see Neveling 2015).

Parallel Trade

It is clear that the politically enforced economic application of neoliberalism's ideology of deregulation, free international trade agreements and the opening up of markets has facilitated and encouraged the global trade in illicit medicines. In the EU internal market, with its lack of restrictions, this process is supported by the flow of products created by the legal practice of parallel trade. There is no space to fully explore the history of parallel trade, which, as part of the move to an EU single market, includes issues of intellectual property (IP), competition and regulatory law. However, it is important to include a brief examination in our analysis of illicit medicine supply.

In short, parallel trade is based on the free movement of trade in the EU internal market and is permitted under Article 28 and 81 of the European Commission Treaty for the Free Movement of Goods and Service within the Internal Market of the EU countries. Parallel trade can be said to be in operation when a product is purchased by a trader in a country where the price is cheaper and re-exported, without the authorisation of the owner of the IP rights, to another country where the product secures a higher price (see Maskus 2002). The trade is 'legal by virtue of the rule of regional exhaustion of trademark rights applied in the EU and the EEA' (EAEPC 2013). However, whereas free trade occurs with the voluntary participation of all parties, parallel trade 'opposes the interests and wishes of the affected manufacturers' (Graham cited in Wagner, no date: 5).

The UK is one of the largest and most lucrative EU markets 'targeted' by parallel pharmaceutical traders, who *legitimately* exploit price differentials between states to profit from countries where higher prices result in higher profit margins. Drawing on data from the British Association of European Pharmaceutical Distributors, the professional body that represents British parallel traders, Morgan (2008) estimates that the parallel pharmaceutical trade in the UK 'is worth 13 per cent of total UK drug sales of £9–10 billion' (Morgan 2008), although the estimate across the EU is much smaller—between two and three per cent.

The European Association of Euro-Pharmaceutical Companies (EAEPC), which represents European parallel traders, states that the parallel pharmaceutical trade in Europe is an 'integral part of the European pharmaceutical market that adds value to society by introducing price competition and a supplementary layer of product safety'. This statement seems to contradict the slogan on their website from a pharmaceutical executive, 'the paramount aim is to go for the best price in every country' (EAEPC 2013). Profit maximisation is legitimated because it is seen as crucial to the functioning of free trade practices in the internal market. Yet in practice parallel traders are pitted against wholesalers and large pharmaceutical companies. As Satchwell notes '[i]n the UK, hospitals and Primary Care Trusts are encouraged by the government, as the monopoly tax-funded payer for services, to buy drugs from the cheapest possible source' and turn to parallel traders in order to do so (2004: 11). The EU commission states that in theory this should reduce prices for the consumer and promote healthy competition. However, the EU's permission given to parallel trade in pharmaceuticals has had an enabling impact on the trade in illicit medicines in a number of ways, one of which is to provide opportunities for counterfeiters, which of course risks the safety of consumers.

Parallel trade incentivises the illegal trade in medicines because the principle of free movement on which the trade is based lifts barriers and opens up competition in prices between states. In effect it also incentivises the counterfeiting of medicines and makes detection more difficult. The process of importing, reimporting, repackaging and reselling provides many opportunities for illicit medicines to enter the legitimate supply chain, offering higher profit margins because the original product will have been bought at a cheaper price. The repackaging process also means 'pristine packaging is available to be used for counterfeit products, although the redundant packaging is *supposed* to be destroyed' (Satchwell 2004: 12, emphasis added). Moreover, trademark owners are prohibited from preventing repackaging of their products if it is deemed to have no adverse effect on the original manufactured goods (see Laing 2005: 852). Therefore, by default the regulatory system condones the passing of medicines through numerous countries and sellers before they reach the final distributor who supplies direct to the consumer. Occasionally legitimate drugs can be replaced with falsified or substandard medicines, or products that have been through a process of 'salting'—whereby legitimate products are bulked out with counterfeit products—while *en route* to another market. Overall, the principle we can draw from this is that the longer the drug distribution channels the more vulnerable the legitimate supply chain becomes and the more opportunities are presented for the supply of illicit medicines.

Actors involved in the illicit medicine trade have recognised the opportunities presented by parallel trade in the EU and practice illegal parallel trade. Morgan reported that the Medicines and Healthcare products Regulatory Agency (MHRA) had recalled nine cases of illicit medicines in the UK over a three-year period and 'a further five cases caught at wholesaler level before they reached the market' (Morgan 2008). Instances of fakes entering the legitimate supply chain in the UK include the most notorious case of illegal parallel trade in pharmaceuticals (see Box 4.6

below). In the summer of 2007 a number of items entered the supply chain as a direct result of parallel trading, including products used to treat psychosis, blood clots and cancer: 'Some 40,000 packs of tablets were seized by the MHRA and up to a further 10,000 were recalled' (ibid). Peter Gillespie—whose defence was that he believed he was involved in a legal parallel trade from France—was convicted as the ringleader of a network involved in one of the most serious breaches of the laws that govern the UK pharmaceutical supply chain. In 2011 he was sentenced to eight years in prison and was recently fined £5.6 million (Gregory 2013). The illicit medicines he sold were packaged in French but had been produced in China and shipped to Singapore. They were then 'bought by a wholesaler in Luxembourg who sold them on to a Belgian wholesaler and another based in Liverpool, who in turn sold them to UK parallel importers' (Morgan 2008). This is one of the *known* cases of illegal parallel trade, highlighting the problems associated with a long and complex distribution chain with little regulation opening up the EU to counterfeiters. This type of business practice, operating largely outside of the new EU legislation on falsified medicines, must be regulated with more vigour if it is to continue without posing serious risks to the health of European citizens.

Our evidence suggests that parallel trade can offer opportunities for criminals involved in illicit medicine distribution, as well as increasing prices by enforcing competition between states in legitimate import–export transactions. These anomalies emphasise the downside and the limits to the free movement of trade, where so-called competition leaves patients open to consuming fakes, and patients in some countries where specific pharmaceutical products sell at a lower price unable to access the products they require as parallel trade creates shortages in supply. For instance, it has been reported that patients in Greece find it more difficult to acquire certain medicines used to treat epilepsy and bipolar disorder because once these products reach the country they are usually re-exported to the UK or Germany for a higher end-price (see Morgan 2008; see also Cassidy 2012). This also presents opportunities for counterfeiters to capture the gap in the market created in Greece, by supplying illicit products in place of the products that are unobtainable through legitimate avenues. In these situations the boundaries between legitimate and illegitimate pharmaceutical supply become indistinct.

Although these instances of fakes entering the legitimate supply chain are not directly related to online sites of supply, digital technologies often aid connections and financial transactions between criminal actors. Moreover, the online market has also been expedited by parallel trade, wherein the complexities and weaknesses in the drug distribution chain are exploited by illegal parallel traders largely involved in selling products over the Internet. Our research indicates that the Internet plays a pivotal role in this illegal trade in the UK and free market principles such as parallel trade increase the commercial opportunities and lower the legal risks associated with it. Therefore, to suggest simply that the online trade in illicit medicines exists outside of legitimate political and economic structures and the pharmaceutical industry is misleading. The trade cannot be regarded as 'outside' of the processes of the legitimate political economy, because within the neoliberal variant of the legitimate political economy enabling structures have been introduced that allow and in some ways tacitly encourage the illegitimate trade in pharmaceuticals to flourish. Both parallel trade within the EU internal market and the shipment of illicit goods entering the UK via historically established trade routes and distribution circuits including SEZs—from Asia and Latin America, through central Europe, the UAE or West Africa—are crucial features of the overall trade in illicit medicines.

OFFLINE PHYSICAL FLOWS: THE CHANNELS AND NETWORKS OF PRODUCTION AND DISTRIBUTION

A variety of channels and networks through which the illicit medicine trade is put into practice have recently established themselves. This reiterates the importance of a discussion of both the virtual and physical elements of the trade and their interconnections. It is generally understood that the trade in illicit medicines follows a common pattern from production and distribution through to consumption. The trade is widely dispersed in geographical space, and the products are manufactured and packaged, often in stages, before being transited and distributed through a variety of trade routes in a complex supply chain, frequently taking advantage of the SEZs situated around the globe. As we have seen, production centres are to be found mainly in South Asia (India, Pakistan and Bangladesh), China, Russia and Latin America, and distribution tends to be at its most active in large networks in parts of the Middle East, Africa and Central Europe. Drawing on data from the OECD, Pryswa points out that '75 % of counterfeit medicines in the world come from China and India and half of these products transit through Dubai to conceal their origin' (IRACM 2013: 18). From the regulatory holes in Chinese manufacturing to the movement of goods through free trade zones in the United Arab Emirates, we have found a variety of geographical zones involved in the trade. Therefore, we propose a zonal model to help determine and understand the operation of the routes through which the physical flows of illicit medicines take place.

Zones of Production

There has been a general shift in the pharmaceutical market, which is re-contextualising and affecting both the legitimate and illegitimate industries. The burgeoning trade in generics is the key priority for large pharmaceutical companies to tackle, while counterfeits in comparison pose a lower risk to their dominant market share (KPMG 2012).

Similarly, suggesting a tangible crossover between legitimate and illegitimate markets, the most significant production hubs involved in the trade of illicit medicines are located in India, Pakistan, China and Hong Kong, where numerous chemical and equipment companies are manufacturing the active pharmaceutical ingredients (APIs) and devices needed to produce illicit medicines. It has been suggested that India is the largest supplier of counterfeit drugs (see Wertheimer and Wang 2012: 6). India is also the world's largest producer of generic drugs, closely followed by China and an increasing contribution from Russia and some Latin American states. We found evidence to suggest other major players involved in this stage of the process are Russia, Nigeria and the Philippines. Nevertheless, clandestine factories have also been found in Ukraine, Indonesia, Thailand, Colombia, Bolivia, Paraguay, Turkey and Iraq.

The rise of newly economically advanced countries, sometimes referred to as BRIC countries, offers distinct economic advantages in terms of the production of medicines. In China and India manufacturing costs are as much as 40 per cent cheaper than competitors in other states because of the relative affordability of labour and resource price differentials. These countries are major commercial platforms where counterfeit products have been historically produced. The large existing legitimate pharmaceutical industries producing generic and branded products in these countries also offer opportunities for counterfeit operations, which, as we have seen, are sometimes illicit operations running alongside legitimate production and distribution processes.

There are various organisational scales of production (see Yar 2008: 154). They range from small-scale operations running from an individual's home, through medium-scale operations including legitimate factories functioning counterfeit operations at night, to large-scale industrial illicit operations or clandestine factories. There are also various and distinct stages in production: the chemical production of APIs, pill pressing, packaging, repackaging and so on. These may be based in one place or in a variety of places. Usually, raw materials/APIs are produced in China and India, but sometimes these materials are then 'smuggled' through porous borders into countries in Africa, Latin America and Eastern Europe for secondary production, which includes pressing pills and packaging. Packaging is of upmost importance, especially for products targeting developed countries such as the UK. Processes of packaging and repackaging are located in various geographic locations, sometimes free zones that lie *en route* as the products are in transit.

Zones of Transit and Distribution

As Wertheimer and Wang point out, the trade in pharmaceuticals includes 'several intermediaries', which 'increases the opportunities for counterfeiters' (2012: 41). The use of shell companies and the Internet and e-commerce in the distribution process is significant (see IRACM 2013: 18; Yar 2008: 157, discussion above). However, in terms of physical flows between the chemical manufacturer, the pharmaceutical producer and the importer country we can find a number of points of transit and distribution, which, with parallel trade in the EU internal market, also means that various avenues are opened up for trade in illicit medicines once products reach the EU.

Our evidence suggests that the following regions are zones of transit and distribution significantly implicated in the illicit medicine trade (this is by no means an exhaustive list):

- The Middle East—the UAE, Jordan and Iraq.
- Central and Eastern Europe—Russia, Kazakhstan and Ukraine.
- West, East and South Africa—Nigeria, Angola, Benin and Cameroon.

We have already noted that a large number of free zones in Nigeria and the UAE have been implicated in the illicit medicine trade. Here we can flesh this out with a little more detail. These free zones are designated

areas, usually ports, with reduced or removed tariffs and duties and relatively lax customs controls. They are ideal locations for counterfeit products to be placed in transit before being distributed around the globe.
With the arrival of the final stage of globalisation in the late twentieth
century, containerisation became a popular means of transiting goods
but also a particularly popular way of concealing and smuggling counterfeit products. This again highlights the essential and ubiquitous links
between legal and illegal in global capitalism as a system of accumulation
(see Nordstrom 2007; Hudson 2015).

In the Middle East, the UAE—and Dubai in particular—as Bogadich
points out, offers

> way stations for goods moving around the globe. Since most of the ship-
> ments do not officially enter the country, there are fewer bureaucratic entan-
> glements. In the emirates' zones, the usual requirement for local ownership
> of companies is waived, and there are no import and export fees or income
> tax. (Bogadich 2007)

Therefore, free trade zones offer the opportunity 'to hide – or sani-
tize – a drug's provenance, or to make, market or re-label adulterated
products' (ibid.). The products are then passed through a multitude
of distribution channels before reaching their destinations. The supply chain of a batch of illicit medicines may start in China and be
transited in Dubai before heading through Caribbean island states to
the USA, to Europe and back again before landing in the UK. These
distribution channels vary and take advantage of porous borders and
container-based shipping. Counterfeiters are aware that the longer the
distribution chain, the harder the products are to detect. Alongside the
shipping industry, a retired customs officer we interviewed revealed
that rail routes into Europe from China are regularly used to transport
containers of illicit medicines, which in the context of the new rail
route connecting China, Kazakhstan, Azerbaijan, Georgia and Turkey,
could significantly increase in the near future (see Port Technology
2015).

Data from open and closed (anonymous) sources, including private
stakeholders and law enforcement, have been used to build the following map to identify zones of production, zones of transit and distribution and common trade routes involved in the illicit medicine trade
(Fig. 4.1):

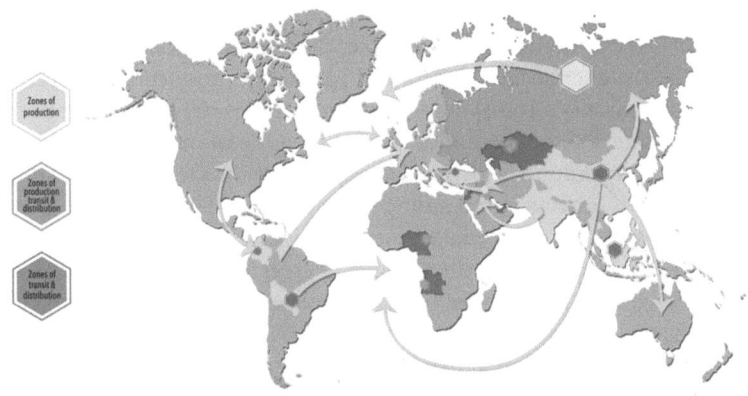

Fig. 4.1 Map highlighting global flows of illicit medicines (*Source*: Authors' research)

THE TRADE'S SOCIAL ORGANISATION

As the book has demonstrated, the online trade in illicit medicines can involve a number of online sites and services to market products and maintain financial flows, as well as a range of channels and networks formed around distribution and production. However, who are the actors involved in the supply and how are they organised? And how can we begin to map out the crossover between the online and offline, legitimate and illegitimate, and global and local in this context?

Actors

A number of actors and various operational structures are involved in the processes of manufacturing, formulating, distributing and selling illegal pharmaceuticals over the Internet. Functional roles range from obtaining raw materials, primary manufacture of APIs, formulation of APIs (drug synthesis) including pressing and coating, and packaging and repackaging, to marketing, advertising, online selling and transportation of the final products. In order to manufacture illicit medicines actors must produce or obtain both the APIs and the packaging that is comparable to popular branded products (Wertheimer and Wang 2012: 2). For large-scale operations this requires a skilled workforce and plants/factories with necessary equipment for the various stages of the production process, and a team of people involved in the distribution of the products both online and offline.

We acknowledge that these roles may shift and may be undertaken by the same actor or organisation—for example, the counterfeiters may run operations where the chemical engineers and packaging producers are located in the same organisation. It may be that an operation is producing and packaging on the same site, or there may be some degree of outsourcing. It could be that a logistics company involved is responsible for a range of tasks during the distribution process, from storage to transport. Finally, we need to be aware that these are commercial enterprises with networks of actors involved during various stages and with varying degrees of transparency. Some of those involved may be unaware of their involvement in an illicit market.

Overall, the actors involved in the illicit medicine trade, excluding the legal pharmaceutical companies whose merchandise is produced legally but traded illegally, are as follows:

1. *Producers:* These individuals and associated organisations are involved in producing (and selling) illicit medicines to wholesalers or criminal entrepreneurs/crime groups, or, less often, in the small-scale selling of their own products over the Internet. Their skills range from amateur to professional:

   a. *Amateurs*—individuals with no formal training possibly buying wholesale online and pressing pills at home to sell to the UK consumers.

   b. *Semi-professionals*—these are not pharmaceutical professionals but have built up the skills to produce a fairly accurate product.

   c. *Professionals*—actual professionals who have become involved in the counterfeit business.

2. *Chemical engineers:* These individuals, usually working on behalf of an API service, are involved in chemical processing and produce and supply the controlled substances. They produce the APIs, but also the substances used as filters or binders to bulk out the medicines. Moreover, enteric coating also needs to be produced (some reports show it tends to be the indigestibility of the coating, not the adulterated APIs, which causes consumers harm when illicit medicines are consumed). Thousands of chemical compounds are used in pharmaceutical production in a variety of forms of drug synthesis. These manufacturing personnel can range from skilled chemists with experience in the industry to those with no skills and experience following recipes/directions, and these services may be clandestine or legitimate. Sometimes the raw materials are shipped to other countries for pressing/production, then to another for packaging/repackaging.

3. *Equipment producers and installers:* Any operation needs specific equipment designed to make the required pharmaceuticals, from basic laboratory equipment to powder blenders and testers, tablet presses and capsule printers. This requires the equipment to be produced and installed by those with the technical knowledge and skills. The equipment and installation in clandestine operations may be carried out by legitimate companies who may know or not know of the illegitimacy of the operation.

4. *Non-specialised workers:* As in most production and distribution businesses, a range of workers are needed for menial tasks at all levels of the operation/s. These might include lifting and moving stock, packing shelves and so on.

5. *Packaging producers:* Including those involved in printing trademarks and barcodes.

6. *Workers in health-related establishments:* Those who are responsible for obtaining merchandise or other materials (e.g. cleaners collecting empty bottles), who may become implicated in supplying packaging materials to counterfeiters.

7. *Transportation intermediaries:* At different stages of the operation, from pre-packaging, post-production and final distribution channels via air, land and sea. For example, freight trucking companies and lorry drivers and pilots (see Kennedy and Wilson 2015 for more on the role of legitimate intermediaries in the transportation of counterfeit goods).

8. *Warehouse/storage providers:* A variety of premises are used to store illicit medicines at their various stages of production and distribution, ranging from warehouses to shipment containers. The providers of these services are implicated in the trade.

9. *Importers:* The procurers and importers funding operations, who buy illicit medicines in bulk, buy numerous domain names acquired from website owners and advertise for web designers and drop shippers. Products can be imported either as bulk active ingredients or in dosage form. One well-documented case in the UK is that of Simon Martin Hickman, who ran a multimillion pound website selling fake pills used to treat sexual dysfunction, along with a variety of other sexual aids. The MHRA seized more than £14 million in assets from this Manchester-based criminal entrepreneur in 2012.

10. *Organised crime groups:* A criminal entrepreneur may be part of a larger organisation that bulk-buys medicines and domain names and use similar OP templates. There are larger organisations known to law enforcement, some with links to the Russian mafia and Chinese triads and so on (see also Bate 2008: 35). In some cases, traditional organised crime groups (OCGs) are hired by legitimate wholesalers and rival pharmaceutical companies in China in order to settle competition between companies (see UNODC 2010).

11. *Intermediaries/brokers:* The middlemen putting relevant people in contact with one another and developing trade and transportation routes. This category can include members of diasporic groups well situated to continue business relations and make new contacts. They may oversee the smooth operation of the business, or may simply put relevant people in contact with one another. Here there can be a crossover with the role of counterfeiters and criminal entrepreneurs. Overall, this group consists of those who are able to see 'social holes' and connect others involved in supply (see IRACM 2013).

12. *Retail sellers:* As opposed to the importers, the majority of the sellers are, what Dorn et al. (1992) call, 'opportunistic irregulars', who have a small opportunity to profit from the business. They include user-sellers.

13. *Shell companies/covers/trading companies:* Commercial organisations that often do not specialise in the medicine trade but act as the cover for illicit medicine supply. For instance, travel companies and fashion accessory companies have been found to be supplying illicit medicines. Some are simply diversifying and medicine is part of a larger racket involving the selling of a variety of illicit goods.

14. *Drop shippers:* A UK-based individual can become involved in the trade as a drop shipper by searching affiliate websites and answering adverts, some simply asking 'do you want to earn money?'. Individuals expressing interest are then sent a template for a website attached to one of a group of domain names bought in bulk by a large criminal operation from a legitimate web-hosting company, along with shipments of illicit medicines, which they then sell in smaller quantities to online customers via their OP or a range of other online sites. The individual drop shipper then begins trading in illicit medicines supplied to their home address by the criminal organisation. They are paid per shipment they make, which height-

ens their desire to sell more. These drop shippers are also involved in rerouting goods in the supply chain (see also Palmer 2013 on the role of drop shippers).

15. *Travellers/smugglers*: Carrying relatively small quantities over borders to be supplied to customers who have bought online.

16. *Illegal parallel traders*: Those illegally involved in buying illicit medicines in one market to sell at a higher price in another. Peter Gillespie was an illegal parallel trader (see discussion above).

17. *Corrupt officials:* This can include corrupt customs officers and border police situated at transit points globally involved in distribution. In free trade zones staff have been known to 'turn a blind eye'.

18. *Postal delivery service:* It guarantees that the merchandise traded online reaches customers in the 'real' world. This is one aspect of the infrastructure that largely involves legitimate companies (the large courier firm FedEx was recently indicted in the USA on charges of conspiracy to deliver illicit pharmaceuticals; see Walker 2014).

19. *Postal workers:* Such as postal delivery workers involved in the transport of wholesale quantities over borders and small-scale amounts sent through national postal routes. The MHRA arrested two postal delivery workers in 2013 involved in distributing unlicensed Indian ED drugs in the UK (Waldron 2013).

20. *Affiliates and sub-affiliate networks:* Commercial entities who act as intermediaries to market the products of larger businesses online and are then paid for each referral their marketing succeeds in capturing (see Chap. 2).

21. *Domain name registrars/web-hosting companies*: There are a number of web-hosting companies specifically implicated in the trade (see Chap. 2). It is from these companies that illegal OPs are made available via the web, and where domain names are bought and registered.

22. *Rogue website designers:* They design the templates to be used by criminal organisations and drop shippers as online pharmacies.

23. *E-commerce merchant traders/Internet merchant account suppliers:* In order to collect payments from customers a payment gateway will be required on the site used for supply, which is a link to a merchant account. These are supplied by merchant service providers include those available from large commercial banks.

24. *Other financial services:* Services such as Western Union or high street banks can be used to collect payment or 'clean up' revenue.
25. *Internet intermediaries, e-commerce sites and social networking sites:* Google, Facebook, Ebay, Twitter and Instagram are used as sites for supply and have become implicated in the trade.
26. *Payment gateways and payment processors:* Which are required for credit card transactions and move money between customer's and merchant's acquiring banks (see Chap. 2).

Case Files

In order to explore the trade's social organisation we analysed a number of investigative case files of UK-based operations under investigation at the MHRA. The following six boxes and proceeding analysis illustrates the significant information we gathered:

Box 4.1 Case Study of a Large-Scale Illicit Medicine Operation

Year(s) of alleged offence: 2004–2011.

In 2004 the MHRA began an investigation into a large and complex business purported to be trading in fishing tackle, electric goods, cosmetics and jewellery. After a number of test purchases were made, they were also found to be selling both unlicensed and counterfeit erectile dysfunction drugs online. It was later found that the same operation was selling counterfeit Viagra and Valium offline.

This was a large operation involving the following day-to-day activities:

- Purchasing stock (from abroad and inside the UK)
- Setting up and maintaining websites used to market and sell medicines
- Renting and running a number of storage units

- Setting up and running a number of distribution centres (packing units used to process and distribute orders)
- Renting offices and purchasing packaging and stationery
- Operating secure mail boxes used by customers to post cash and postal orders
- Opening and operating merchant banking facilities, which allowed customers to purchase online by credit and debit card (providers included Cardnet, Streamline and Global Payment Services)
- Setting up and running front companies used to provide any requested documentation required by the bank(s)
- Setting up off-shore banking facilities used to launder money

This case study is particularly interesting in terms of the information that was made available relating to the social organisation of the operation:

- The operation was described as a 'jigsaw of individuals', male and female, who were members of a close knit group of family members and friends.
- Twenty-one suspects were based in two teams. One in the North of England (Humberside, Lincolnshire) and another in the South of England (Brighton, London, Essex). Furthermore, a number of suspects who are yet to be charged are known to be living in Thailand, Greece, Turkey and Spain.
- The units and businesses implicated in the operation were based throughout the UK and the accounts and banking facilities across the globe.

Suspects had obtained a large amount of revenue from the illegal sale of medicines. Evidence gathered highlighted: (1) £11 million in various bank accounts; (2) Receipts showing an average turnover of £60,000 per week, suggesting an annual turnover of £3 million.

Source: MHRA files

Box 4.2 Case Study of an Online Scheme Trading in Illicit Erectile Dysfunction Products

Year(s) of alleged offence: ongoing.

Intelligence gathered by the MHRA as part of Operation Pangea indicates that two suspects are involved in an operation selling a wide variety of unlicensed and counterfeit erectile dysfunction medicines and oral jellies from the premises of a newsagent in Glasgow, Scotland. Covert test purchases were made via telephone and payments made by credit card via the store's PayPoint machine. Furthermore, the same suspects are known to be selling falsified medicinal products on the following online sites:

- Amazon.com
- Glasgow.craigslist.co.uk
- iOffer.com
- familystores.webs.com (this was a website set up by the suspects to sell both unlicensed and counterfeit erectile dysfunction medicines)

Two main suspects, both male. The first owns the premises above and is more heavily implicated in the day-to-day activities. The second owns accounts showing financial transaction are being made to him.

They are supplied by a wholesaler based in China. Suspect marketed products and completed orders via online wholesalers, classified advertising, their own website and over email using PayPal. Falsified medicinal products were also sold over the telephone and in the shop belonging to suspect 1 using the shop's PayPoint machine.

Source: MHRA files

Box 4.3 Case Study of Falsified Erectile Dysfunction Medicines Trafficking

Year(s) of alleged offence: 2003–2007.

An MHRA investigation made a number of test purchases of counterfeit and unlicensed erectile dysfunction drugs from a UK-based website. It was found that the main suspect operated a business called 'MSH World Traders', supplying products to the UK and abroad via the Internet and in the press.

- He operated three linked companies: the online pharmaceutical business, an Indian call centre and a business selling quad bikes.
- He opened a PO Box and received orders and cheques.
- He had opened bank accounts in England, Malta and The Isle of Man that were used to receive cheque and credit card payments.
- He transferred proceeds to various bank accounts overseas.
- Various payments to pharmaceutical suppliers were found.
- The falsified medicinal products being sold were manufactured in India.
- Turnover was calculated at £6,813,155.54 in the period 1.10.03–12.11.07
- In 2012 the MHRA recovered assets totalling £14.4 million from the suspect—the biggest in the organisations history.
- The suspect had been enjoying a lavish lifestyle and owned holiday homes, property in London and luxury cars.
- The suspect pleaded guilty in 2009. His original sentence was ten months; this was later extended to two years to include money laundering charges.

Source: MHRA files

Box 4.4 Case Study of Steroid Trafficking

Year(s) of alleged offence: 2007–2010.

A police investigation found two suspects selling anabolic steroids and prescription-only medicines (POMs) both online and from a gym in Essex between 2007 and 2010. Suspect 1 (who had been prosecuted in the past in relation to similar offences) ran and owned a gym in Essex frequented by those interested in bodybuilding. He began selling anabolic steroids and other prescription drugs he sourced from China to customers in his gym and over the

(continued)

Box 4.4 (continued)

Internet on his own website. The business was purported to be selling protein shakes and other supplements. He also set up merchant banking facilities to receive payments. His website was hosted by EKMpowershop and banking facilities by Barclaycard. Suspect 2 was an associate of suspect 1 and worked in his gym. He also set up his own website to conduct similar activities. He would eventually buy suspect 1's online business for £15,000. Across the period of supply at least 4234 orders worth £413,156.68 were made for class C drugs (steroids) and 471 orders for POMs worth £45,966.75.

Source: MHRA files

Box 4.5 Case Study of Trafficking Operation Dealing in Illicit Lifestyle Medicines

Year(s) of alleged offence: 2011.

In 2011 the UK Border Agency began inspecting consignments destined for three separate addresses in the UK; first in London and second in Loughborough. The packages were being sent from an address in India. This led to the arrest of two male suspects who were charged in December 2013 under The Trade Mark Act and The Medicines Act. Both defendants were part of a large-scale conspiracy to import unlicensed and counterfeit medicines used to treat erectile dysfunction and hair loss into the UK, with some for further onward distribution to other parts of Western Europe. Both defendants were students at Loughborough University and had previously shared an address. A third female suspect was also a previous Loughborough student now living in London (at the London address implicated in the case) who the main suspects paid £50 per week as a drop shipper to receive packages. A further two suspects were interviewed and found to be drop shippers being sent orders by the main perpetrators to redirect to other parts of the EU. The suspects were selling to customers and conversing with numerous suppliers via a number of email addresses. Evidence found that they were in correspondence with a man in The Netherlands who they were distributing products to. Western Union had been used for payments. One male was suspected to be the owner or partner of a factory in Baroda, India being used to supply the products.

Seizures took place in three addresses and uncovered: 62,000 tablets of all four falsified medicinal products at the London address; 3500 Sildenafil, 2800 Tadalafil and 9000 Finasteride at one Loughborough address; 33,800 ED drugs at the second Loughborough address. The total value of the products recovered was £610,000.

Source: MHRA files

Box 4.6 Case Study of Illegal Parallel Trade

Year(s) of alleged offence: 2006–2007.

The MHRA was involved in a 3 ½ year investigation into a conspiracy to import counterfeit prescription medicines from the Far East and insert them into the regulated EU supply chain, particularly the UK, between December 2006 and May 2007. This was a sophisticated conspiracy masterminded by one key suspect, involving manufacture in China of a number of falsified medicinal products that were packaged in French. They included high demand, expensive and life-saving medicines. The products were shipped via Hong Kong to Singapore and Belgium, and then onto the UK where they were further labelled with French vignettes and sold to licensed wholesalers as French stock for relabelling in English for the UK market, before being sold to UK pharmacies. A licensed (re) packager noticed a mistake on a batch number and reported it to the MHRA. Eli Lilly was already involved in an independent investigation into the Chinese manufacturer with the assistance of American LEAs.

This was a huge case spanning a number of years, transactions, companies and individuals. The main suspect was involved with a number of pharmaceutical companies and transactions from approved parallel importing to cover companies set up in the Ivory Coast, which were all done with his business partner (his brother). He also dealt with an international tax adviser based at a firm in

(continued)

Box 4.6 (continued)

Luxembourg, who set up a secret offshore and confidential company run by a trust, with some transactions also involving trading in high value cars. The same company bought goods from a Mauritian-based company, who then supplied the suspect's associates. Various legal and grey market pharmaceutical companies were involved with the suspect over the years. He lived a lavish lifestyle, although having declared bankruptcy.

It is thought 72,000 packs of falsified medicinal products entered the UK as part of the operation out of which 40,000 were seized by the MHRA, 7000 were further recovered and 25,000 reached pharmacies and patients.

Twelve countries were involved in the case, with 93 witnesses from six countries and 205 witness statements given to investigators. The main suspect was sentenced to eight years after a 4 ½ month Crown Court trial. The Chinese manufacturer was sentenced to 6 ½ years in the USA.

Source: MHRA files

The MHRA's investigative case files suggest that the majority of cases involve the online sale of falsified erectile dysfunction medicines, aside from Case 4 (involving steroids and supplements) and Case 6 (the illegal parallel trade in cancer and anti-psychotic medicines). Furthermore, the files suggest that often both counterfeit and falsified medicinal products are sold by the same operation. They also allow us to make a number of observations regarding the organisation of the online trade in illicit medicines in the UK. Firstly, the social organisation of the operations presented highlight that connections are often made between friends, business partners and/or family members. For example, Case 1 was a network of various family members and friends, Case 4 involved two friends/business partners and Case 5 involved friends who had met as students at university. Case 1 is particularly interesting in this regard and offers great insight into the social organisation of one operation involving a large group of friends and family members acting as teams situated in different geographical locations in the UK, alongside others living abroad whose bank accounts would be used to launder money. Secondly, this case also offers interesting details of the operational structure: the different roles played by each individual and team, whether that be purchasing stock from abroad, operating storage and packing units, supporting and maintaining the ICTs used to advertise and trade online or setting up and running front companies.

Another pattern emerges from the data: all cases of online trade in illicit medicines reveal examples of opportunistic crime (see Ruggiero 2000). These individuals and groups already had some of the necessary infrastructure in place—businesses, contacts in the pharmaceutical industry, payment facilities and so on—to assist them in the supply of falsified medicinal products. For example, Case 2 involved a shop with payment facilities available; Case 3 operated an online pharmacy alongside an Indian call centre and another retail business; Case 4 involved gym owners/business partners who saw the opportunity to sell steroids and related prescription drugs used to 'bulk up' to customers at their gym before expanding their business online; Case 5 involved students, one suspected of operating a pharmaceutical production factory in India; and Case 6 where the defendant—Peter Gillespie—was already involved in the pharmaceutical industry, operated companies he could use as fronts and was well versed in the use of offshore banking. Therefore, suppliers involved in the online trade in illicit medicines often see opportunities to sell falsified medicinal products online through their day-to-day business activities and often use infrastructure they already have in place to begin trading.

A number of further observations can be made:

- These existing businesses (gyms, shops and online shops) are used as front companies and existing payment facilities used for the illegal sale of medicines.
- In terms of payments, e-commerce has simplified the process of buying and selling illicit goods, but also borrowing/renting the bank accounts of friends and family members and setting up offshore banking facilities are commonly used to obscure the paper trail in the context of online trade in illicit medicines.
- The profits largely outweigh the risks for suppliers. There were large profits reported in Cases 1, 3 and 6 in particular, and these defendants were leading lavish lifestyles as a result of the trade.
- Various online sites and payment facilities are simultaneously used by the same operation to sell falsified medicinal products. Case 2, for

example, traded via email, a personal website set up as on OP, classified advertising sites and well-known online marketplaces.

• All sales are not necessarily completed online (Case 1, Case 6) and
  there is often a blurred distinction between online and offline processes in the context of the online trade in illicit medicines. The
  Internet, therefore, acts as a force multiplier (Yar 2006: 10) in terms
  of the advertising and marketing function and ease of setting up
  sites and completing commercial transactions, yet offline and online
  worlds constantly collide.

Finally, although in general the case files provided us with little evidence relating to the production stage or from where and from whom the
suppliers were buying their products (usually outside of UK jurisdiction),
Cases 3, 4 and 5 in particular highlighted that Chinese and Indian operations were heavily implicated in the production process. This was also cor-
roborated in interviews with the MHRA—China, India and Pakistan are
the production zones consistently providing UK-based operations with
illicit medicinal products. Therefore, although these cases from the UK
law enforcement are solely related to the UK-based groups and activities, global connections are necessary in order to obtain the products
to sell and the channels and networks of the physical flows of falsified
medicinal products are just as significant to our analysis of the online trade
in illicit medicines. Indeed, in many instances those who produce and
trade illicit medicines offline buy their primary materials online so their
(offline) business is simply an extension of the online supply chain (see
Management Today 2013).

Organisation

Frequently, the supply of counterfeit goods is seen in the context of 'transnational organised crime and illicit global markets'. However, simply con-
ceiving these markets as the sole business of the sort of hierarchical and
stable criminal groups depicted in public discourse, separated out from
the glocal (Hobbs 1998) structures of the political economy, is inaccurate.
The global 'shadow economy' operates through networks and scales just
as the global political economy does more generally, and specific politico-
economic structures and institutions have expanded the opportunities
for actors involved in illegal markets. The relationship between criminal
and legal organisations and the political-economic context of the trade
has been explored earlier, but now it is necessary to draw upon some of

the existing literature to briefly outline the relationship between criminal organisations and the (online) supply of illicit medicines.

The concept of 'organised crime' has no universally accepted defini-tion.[1] As Hetzer points out, '[t]he term represents a complex, intricate, diffuse field of structures, communities and activities, extending into many areas of crime' (2002: 317). A thorough examination of such complexity is beyond the scope of this book (see, however, von Lampe 2016 for an excellent account of organised crime; see also von Lampe 2005). However, if we focus down on counterfeiting, Guarnieri and Przyswa (2013:220), drawing on the work of Monnet and Véry (2010), posit three 'organisa-tional models of counterfeiting related to "real" flows'. The first model highlights instances in which legitimate businesses participate in 'unfair competition by not respecting intellectual property rights'. The second is one in which 'legal companies produce fake goods and work with trans-national criminal businesses that transport and distribute the counterfeit products', and in the third model the counterfeiting business is essen-tially a criminal operation 'controlled by one or more organised criminal groups' (ibid.). Furthermore, IRACM note a variety of criminal organisa-tions that operate in the counterfeit medicine trade, all of which vary in scale, the time they have been involved in the field and whether or not they are operating online (2013: 35). We have found instances of all three models, working across different sites, scales and networks. Therefore, we found it useful to categorise operations according to their business model they have adopted and developed (see Hall and Antonopoulos 2015), which includes:

1. 'Entities' trading exclusively offline in the 'real' world;
2. 'Entities' that were originally involved in the trade offline, but have now moved online to distribute their merchandise; and
3. 'Entities' that focus their skills exclusively in the virtual world.

As the Internet has developed across the globe, we can begin to see a changing dynamic in criminal organisation and the counterfeit trade. We have found that the actors involved do not form 'transnational crimi-nal organisations' working collectively and constantly, although these types of organisation may become involved at some point or may oversee operations. Instead, the organisational models suggested earlier run on a continuum and form dispersed and adaptable networks of actors and organisations often lying at the margins of legitimacy.

In conversation with LEAs it became clear that although the initial production of illicit medicines is widely understood to be the work of chemical companies in China and India, little is known about the 'big players'—counterfeiters and criminal entrepreneurs. Some are known to enforcement agencies but consistently prove to be extremely difficult to track down (e.g. GlavMed). However, the above cases relate to the UK-based operations, not the wider producers and distributors of falsified medicinal products abroad. Overall, there are various structures and scales of operations; some are larger nationally based 'criminal organisations' with international links, others small-scale locally based groups or individuals. Therefore, the presence of OCGs can only be identified in the loosest sense, but that it not to say some concentrated power and reach in the market is not present.

Actors using social media are small-scale amateur sellers, sometimes also users/consumers of prescription drugs, a 'virtual' role that seems to mimic the 'real' street-level dealers involved in illicit drug distribution. As we have highlighted the use of affiliate and sub-affiliate networks can play a significant role in these operation where similar templates are used and users redirected to the webpages from a variety of online searches (see Chap. 2). Therefore, small-scale sellers may be linked to a larger OCGs, although they may have only been connected virtually, a preferred relation because the Internet offers a certain degree of anonymity to sellers as well as consumers. As previous research has shown, in some cases high-volume traders are selling in teams and/or are involved in the supply of falsified medicinal products as part of wider drug supply schemes (Siva 2010). It is also worth reiterating another earlier finding in this broader context—practices of digital prosumption are evident in this context, where we found online user/sellers on Facebook explicitly talking about their avenues of supply (see Chap. 3). One seller was buying wholesale via TradeIndia from an individual based in Tibet. These individuals are essentially bypassing criminal brokers and do not rely on the criminal organisations acting as middle men to supply drop shippers. They may press the pills themselves—the equipment for which is also available via online wholesale sites—and run small operations in the UK. However, in some cases high-volume traders are linked to operations running thousands of affiliate sites, yet few anchor sites.

In the steroids market in particular a loose social organisation of supply was evident among user-sellers. This revolves around individuals who are regulars in gyms and participants in the bodybuilding/power-lifting/fighting scene, who consume *and* sell steroids primarily to friends and other bodybuilders. The large number of steroid sellers who are also users is a feature that greatly affects the steroids trafficking business, especially at the local level. There are many instances in which additional 'layers' are added to the process of distribution as a result of the large number of individual user-sellers obtaining merchandise (online and offline), and supplying small quantities to friends and acquaintances. This trend of 'social supply' has been identified in other substance markets (see, e.g. Pearson and Hobbs 2001; Chatwin and Potter 2014; Moyle and Coomber 2015). These user-sellers enjoy a higher status among bodybuilders because they are seen as facilitators of their muscular development and improvement, as one of our interviewees suggested: 'you get dealer kudos, if you can be the one to "sort me out"'. The Internet opens up opportunities for such non-expert suppliers (see Fincoeur et al. 2014) active in the steroid market but it also offers opportunities for globally dispersed individuals to build relationships and share experiences and knowledge on product types and administration techniques. For example, our research also highlighted virtual relationships being formed on social networking sites, where a certain level of trust was built between buyer and seller over time, which in some respects mimics offline mentoring relationships and distribution patterns we found during the offline ethnography (see Antonopoulos and Hall 2016).

The organisational structures of the actors involved, as we outlined above, are best understood in terms of flexible networks. Criminals involved in the trade form complex and often hard-to-detect networked structures. Links are made between actors involved in both offline and online activities related to the trade at various operational stages and in different geographical locations. These connections can form information networks, manufacturing networks and (sub)networks within networks. These fluid networks of actors are working in the context of global trade liberalisation and the rise of the Internet and e-commerce. Strategic planning is practiced, but operations and networks are constantly shifting and at times appear to be unstructured. Organisation is necessary in order to generate revenue. Therefore, this is an example of organised crime in the loose sense of a fragmented organisational structure. It requires some degree of organisation, yet the individuals involved are often outsourced (see ASMAG 2012) and loosely networked. Although some may fund the crime in the first instance and profit the most, various dispersed individuals are connected in the overall operation. In this way it mirrors the legitimate supply chain in terms of global trade relations, business transactions and employment relations in a neoliberal economy.

In the context of outsourcing in the pharmaceutical industry, the trade utilises a number of third parties in the process of manufacturing APIs and packaging, usually operating in countries 'that are politically stable and have cheap and skilled labour and a favourable tax regime' (Satchwell 2004: 9). As Satchwell points out, this process 'involves the sharing of valuable information about the exact design and construction of drugs', which counterfeiters use to produce illicit medicines. Wertheimer and Wang label these 'inferior ghost factories', typically legitimate operations running an illegitimate sister company during the night (2012: 2). This is one reason why complicity is crucial to our understanding. After all, without the involvement of legal companies this trade could not take place. We have found large packaging and laboratory equipment companies and chemical companies who are not screening customers, although some regulation was in the early stages of being introduced. This opens up various opportunities for illegitimate actors to buy from legal companies. This is not just a case of an illegal trade emerging in the shadows of a legal trade, but of the boundaries between legal and illegal businesses becoming blurred in various stages of the production and distribution process.

Furthermore, while in many cases the activities of counterfeiters can be seen in light of the literature on 'transnationalism'—in as much as they encompass a multiplicity of interactions and linkages of individuals and institutions across the borders of nation states—they also have national and local manifestations, with communities and criminals positioned globally in order to maintain the smooth running of a complex supply chain. As Hobbs (1998) notes, flexibility and adaptability of criminal practices are necessities in an era of unfettered global capitalism, but transnationalism should not detract from situated locales and local interests. Criticising the work on transnationalism as lacking a conception of the nation state and locales functioning within them, he argues that '[i]t is at the local level that organised crime manifests itself as a tangible process of activity' (1998: 408). Therefore, modern criminality lies at the dialectic between the global and the local. More recently, and specifically in the context of counterfeiting and cybercrime, Treadwell supports this contention: 'The commonly held perception of both types of offending suggest that it is controlled by organised criminal syndicates, yet clearly such crime likely runs a continuum from the macro level of the sophisticated counterfeiting cartel through to the micro level of neighbourhood and localised criminal actors' (2011: 177). This seems to suggest that an appropriate analytical framework can be found in the work on glocalisation, in which an attempt is made to 'recast' global processes as existing on various yet simultaneous 'spatial scales' (see Swyngedouw 2004: 25).

In the context of the online trade in illicit medicines, we have found the local to be of significance in terms of tracing the activities of individual criminal entrepreneurs, and in contextualising small-scale operations in spaces connecting producers, distributors and consumers positioned in different national and local settings. However, we have also witnessed a heightened degree of anonymity offered by virtual spaces that has weakened this sense of locale. Alongside the Internet and e-commerce, modern postal and transport systems and the deregulated conduits of global trade have now compressed spatial and temporal features of criminal markets in the field of commercial transactions. Some criminal actors involved in the trade—although they function in collaboration with networks of other actors—never physically meet their suppliers or customers and exchange data and facilitate financial transactions from the privacy of their own homes. These individuals and groups can then build flexible underground networks with ease (see also Castells 2010). Moreover, commodities move freely through liberalised and unrestricted spaces. Here, it is important to identify the role of legitimate businesses and abstract processes of the global political economy. After all, transnationally, nationally and/or locally manifested criminal activities do not exist in a vacuum, but accompany overarching processes of neoliberal globalisation.

'Pay as You Grow:' The Online Trade in Illicit Medicines as the By-Product of Contemporary Dynamics in the Legal Pharmaceutical Industry

It is widely known that the western legal pharmaceutical industry (the big, multinational companies) faces numerous challenges with the most important one being blockbuster medicines losing patent protection and going generic, the arrival of generic price competition, and the pressure to invest more on innovation in order for new blockbuster medicines to be created (Gupta et al. 2010; Hemphill and Sampat 2012; Shares 2013). In order to preserve profit margins these western companies outsource research and manufacturing to China, primarily, and India. In 2009, for example, AstraZeneca decided to move all production to China "as part of its cost-cutting drive" (Ahmed 2009: 126).

All major pharmaceutical companies have already rushed to invest in China in order to take advantage of the relatively low cost of employees, the presence of good scientists and the great potential of the Chinese pharmaceutical market primarily because of its size (Ahmed 2009). This process, which involved acquisition of even big Chinese companies by the western Big Pharma (Einhorn et al. 2011), was coupled by the Chinese government's 12th Five-Year Plan (2011–2015) that involved pushing towards consolidation and industrial advancement through eliminating outdated and excessive capacity in the pharmaceutical industry and beyond (Deloitte 2011). In this context, for instance, Zhejiang Hangzhou Xinfu Pharma wholly acquired other important Chinese companies such as Hefei Yifan Biopharma and Hefei Yifan Pharma (China Pharmaceutical and Biotechnology Review 2013a, b). On other occasions, multinational pharmaceutical companies and Chinese companies launched joint ventures such this by Pfizer and Zhejiang Hisu (First World Pharma 2012; see also Garde 2013).

These developments however had a number of adverse effects on the Chinese pharmaceutical industry that are relevant to the counterfeiting business. The most important one is that in the process of consolidation and eliminating excess, a significant number of the employees of these companies were made redundant (China Pharmaceutical and Biotechnology Review 2013a), a practice that is also apparent in the West (see Neate and Farrell 2014). Amongst this group a significant number of skilled scientists (pharmacists, chemical engineers, biotechnologists, etc.) became unemployed and available to the counterfeiting business.

Secondly, these developments cut to a significant extent the links between the *extremely* fragmented pharmaceutical market (at the level of production) and the hundreds of thousands of small-scale retailers and distributors at the end of the supply chain (Kimes 2010; Shank 2010; see also Wei 2013). Similar fragmentation of the retail marker and a large number of (often unregistered) independent small pharmacies that are inadequately supervised is the case in countries such as India and Pakistan (see Chowdhury 2010; see also CIPHP 2007). These businesses, which are often small, family-run businesses, are now faced with significant challenges other than the fierce competition of local competitors; challenges such as limited cash flow and survival (see Tse et al. 2012; Saini et al. 2011) in light of the unaffordability caused not only by the limited buying power of a significant part of the local population but also the heavy duties and taxes on retail medicines, which can be as much as 55 per cent (see Morris and Stevens 2006). There are two ways out of this hardship: firstly, diversification, that is, selling a wide range of commodities (along with medicines), and, secondly, expanding the pool of potential customers by going online and reaching customers in the international market for pharmaceuticals. The appropriation of e-commerce may be having a scaling effect that allows petty pharmaceutical traders in Asia to act globally. This is a form of innovation on the part of small pharmaceutical traders that counterbalances the forms of 'innovation' that the Big Pharma has in its arsenal, which, other than expanding to a new market on the other side of the globe, include 'evergreening' as well as using their financial and political capital (the most prominent example is Novartis) to block the production on generic pharmaceuticals (see Exantas 2013; Harvey 2012) that could serve poor consumers.

This 'extroversion' of small entrepreneurs (both producers and retailers) is also facilitated by the relevant legal frameworks in these major producers of counterfeit medicines such as China and India. In 2012, for instance, the Chinese government amended its patent laws to allow Chinese pharmaceutical companies to reproduce generic, low-cost versions of expensive western medicines for the national market and to export them in various contexts including the Western world (Huff 2012). In India, legal pharmaceutical companies are allowed by law to manufacture counterfeit drugs if these are destined for foreign markets. If these medicines are destined for the Indian market the activity is illegal (JDSU 2010). It is, therefore, unsurprising that, according to the US Chamber of Commerce, India and China are consistently the worst in patent theft and copyright infringement (Hofmann 2013).

One always needs to remember that although in the West innovation means launching new consumers goods and services, in China, India and other Asian countries innovation is celebrated as 'the bettering of *existing* process' and commodities (Mallick 2013; emphasis added). In this context counterfeiting is generally tolerated as a 'normal' economic activity and dealt with rather leniently in the legal sphere. In China, as Bronshtein has argued, penalties for illegal pharmaceutical production 'are considered a mere cost of doing business … rather than a deterrent from engaging in counterfeiting' (2008: 439).

CONCLUSION

The few existing analyses of pharmaceutical falsification tend to associate the trade with 'organised crime'. However, the limited focus of mainstream accounts frequently omits the crucial facilitating components of the structures and processes of the global political economy, the simultaneous global and local manifestations of the crimes, and the often 'disorganised' and fluid patterns and routes through which these activities take place. Instead—along with evidence of a diverse and flexible nature to the types of criminal organisation involved in the online trade in illicit medicines—this chapter has shown that the supply of illicit medicines is entrenched in global variations in IPR, the blurred boundaries of the legitimate and illegitimate pharmaceutical industries, the global free market and transnational trade relations.

Although our research focuses specifically on the online trade, we have found the online and offline elements of the trade are inextricably linked. The communications revolution and the ensuing global reach of the Internet has facilitated a huge expansion in opportunities for geographically dispersed criminal actors involved in the illicit medicine trade. Not only marketing and selling, but production and distribution processes are facilitated by the Internet, e-commerce and modern ICTs. However, as we have shown, the channels and networks of the physical flows of illicit medicines are just as significant to our analysis, from the use of SEZs, historically established trade routes and modern transport facilities, to the simultaneous global, national and local scales in which these processes occur. Overall, the supply of illicit medicines is embedded in inseparable and interrelated political forces, economic processes and technological advancements that blur the boundaries of legality, but it is also socially and culturally rooted, requiring the formation of networks of actors situated on a range of sites.

NOTE

1. Klaus von Lampe has collated some 180 definitions of organised crime on his website: www.organized-crime.de.

CHAPTER 5

Conclusion

Abstract This chapter offers concluding remarks, tying together the research on demand and supply with an analytical framework that considers the constitutive function of a number of complex and interdependent processes, structures and spaces. This highlights the multilayered and often contradictory nature of the online trade in illicit medicines. Studying the actor's involved, their networks and illicit practices, often blurs the distinctions between various concepts: political economy and culture; legality and illegality; online and offline; and global and local. It is argued that an analysis of the trade must be positioned in a critical discussion of late-modern capitalist dynamics and processes of accumulation.

Keywords online/offline • global/local • neoliberalism

The online trade in illicit medicines in the UK is a growing and under-researched criminological phenomenon. Actors in the trade are involved in the production, distribution and consumption of counterfeit, substandard, unlicensed and illegally supplied pharmaceutical products. The trade is multilayered and often contradictory. It is also embedded in a number of complex and interdependent processes, structures and spaces. Studying

© The Author(s) 2016   113
A. Hall, G.A. Antonopoulos, *Fake Meds Online*,
DOI 10.1057/978-1-137-57088-8_5

actor's networks and illicit practices within and between them often blurs the distinctions between various concepts: political economy and culture; legality and illegality; online and offline; and global and local. Accordingly, this book borrows theories and concepts from criminology, critical political economy, consumer culture, medical sociology and digital/new media studies to advance a new transdisciplinary analytical lens through which to understand the trade. This analytical approach is grounded on an integrated and innovative research methodology comprised of online and offline ethnographies—which include interviews and observations with active criminal entrepreneurs, consumers of illicit medicines, private stakeholders and enforcement officers—analyses of investigative case files, and various secondary media and academic sources.

To summarise the basic structure of the argument, Chap. 1 introduced the analytical approach and summarised the methodology. This was followed by three substantive chapters based on the research findings. Chapter 2 examined the online trade in illicit medicines in the UK. First, it offered a brief history of pharmaceutical falsification. The focus was the political, economic and technological shifts that have facilitated a monumental growth in the illicit medicine trade in the twenty-first century. Second, the chapter explored the distinct characteristics of the trade in the UK, which acts as both a transit zone and end-user market targeted by illicit medicine suppliers looking to attach legitimacy to parcels heading to other markets, or to cash in on the UK's relatively lucrative consumer market. As we explored the distribution of the most popular illicit medicines currently being bought online by the UK consumers, and the legal and regulatory framework currently in place to target suppliers, we found a number of regulatory and legal loopholes that have a formative effect on the increasing popularity of this market among criminal entrepreneurs. Finally, the chapter examined the Internet infrastructure required to trade in illicit medicines online, which includes a number of tools, services and tactics, including an increasingly significant role played by user-generated content.

Drawing on data from the virtual and offline ethnographies, Chap. 3 explored the consumer demand in more depth and detail. First, we contextualised the UK consumer/patient in the virtual world. Next, we offered an advanced understanding of the consumer decision-making processes and other contributing factors that influence the purchase of medicines online, prominent amongst which are the increasingly privatised culture of pharmaceutical consumption, the avoidance of stigma and pharmaceutical drug diversion. This revealed that a number of social groups in the UK are particularly at risk of buying and consuming illicit medicines online—students and teenagers, individuals suffering from mental health problems, self-defined 'expert patients' self-diagnosing online, various individuals seeking lifestyle drugs for cosmetic/aesthetic reasons, women seeking lower costs on fertility treatments and bodybuilders looking to 'bulk up' (see Antonopoulos and Hall 2016). Distribution of illicit medicines to these groups was theorised in the broad contexts of (1) changing cultures of pharmaceutical consumption and healthcare practice, and (2) the effects of digital technologies operating in broader politico-economic structures and processes. For instance, our research emphasised the active role Web 2.0 and participatory online networks plays in facilitating and normalising online pharmaceutical consumption. These consumption practices have been further energised by an increasingly marketised National Health Service and desires from the new cultural norm of the self-governing expert patient.

Chapter 4 focused on the supply side and examined the dynamics shaping the physical flows of illicit medicines around the world. First, we explored the political economy of supply, which exposed the use of historically established trade routes, SEZs and parallel trading practices in the illicit pharmaceutical supply chain. Second, we proposed a zonal model that outlined the most regularly utilised channels and routes through which illicit medicines are produced and distributed. Third, the chapter explored the social organisation of the illicit medicine trade. The data from investigative case files were presented and, along with other sources, highlighted the key actors involved in the trade in the UK, their motivations, how they are organised and how the trade can be conceptualised as a by-product of the legal industry.

Throughout the research we found that the trade's material and financial flows are entrenched in the structures of the global political economy and global supply chains. In the current neoliberal era unregulated wholesale systems, misguided trade barriers, variations in intellectual property laws, and the differential characteristics of producer and consumer economies (see Passas 1999) encourage the supply of illicit medicines. The trade is contingent on porous borders and trade routes, and it has become more widespread and intense as a direct result of the deregulation of international trade and liberalisation of financial markets from the 1980s. Indeed, the financial centres of the world compete for the capital return of criminal enterprise. Ever since the abolition of many capital exchange controls, the offshore banking industry has been able to 'clean up' and store accumulated assets (Shaxson 2011; Hudson 2015). This is just one of the entry points through which 'legitimate' businesses and economic institutions can become implicated in this 'illegitimate' trade.

Neoliberalism's political economy is attended by a culture that is increasingly individualised, commodified and medicalised. It has normalised the consumer's search for pharmaceuticals outside legitimate avenues. The search is supported by an evolving technological infrastructure (see Beer 2013) that acts to obscure the previously separate spheres of production and consumption in the context of the online medicine trade. Such technology offers actors, who are at once producers, distributors and users, a space in which to do business and share their consumption experiences and healthcare practices. The digital world presents networking opportunities for suppliers of illicit medicines as it expands opportunities for both dispersal *and* concentration. In the context of the illicit online medicine trade we have found high-volume and globally dispersed suppliers, as well as highly concentrated schemes operating on a wider scale, whose actors often have a fair amount of IT knowledge and skill, or a team to which IT services can be contracted out. However, despite the 'transnationality' of this illegal market, our investigation has shown that it also has *national* and *local* manifestations. Overall, the trade's suppliers and their operations exist on varied yet simultaneous scales; some are larger criminal organisations with pockets of concentrated power and reach (e.g. GlavMed), while others are small-scale nationally or locally based groups or individuals.

The detached and dispersed nature of e-commerce and the flexibility of the criminal organisations involved pose huge research problems, so research tends to become absorbed in their study. This diverts the attention of the criminological research community from the roles that various legal trading companies play in the trade. Throughout this research, however, we unearthed numerous ways in which the trade is entrenched in the extralegal (Nordstrom 2007; see also Hall 2012). Our research has shown that the trade is illustrative of the counter geographies of globalisation (Sassen 1998): the dynamic and fluid networks and flows that are to a considerable extent part of the informal economy, but also use sectors of the legal economy's infrastructure and support across various spatial scales. This is particularly apparent when we consider social media and their role in advertising and marketing illicit medicines, as well as payment processors, gateways and the acquiring banks that manage the financial flows and the proceeds of crime. This issue is mirrored in the offline aspects of the trade. For instance, alongside those supporting the digital infrastructure, legitimate intermediaries are used for production and transportation purposes. In many instances we have found legitimate and illegitimate companies in both online and offline contexts becoming associates—whether knowingly or not—in the illicit medicine trade.

At every point in the supply chain we have found some sort of formative role played by the legal industry. The nature and dynamics of the legal pharmaceutical industry in the context of global capitalism has bolstered the illegal industry that has emerged in its shadow, in many respects calling into question our ability to draw a clear distinction between the illegitimate and legitimate industries. In the context of the formation of a financial imbalance among big, medium and small pharmaceutical firms throughout the globe—specifically between the big pharmaceutical companies of the West and the pharmaceutical companies in contexts such as India and China—the illegal online trade in medicines is often the product of the pre-emptive fear of the legal pharmaceutical firms and retailers 'not making it' and losing their fingerhold on the pharmaceutical industry (see also Antonopoulos and Hall 2014). Pharmaceutical companies (producers and retailers) compete hard in the industry. With such a powerful amoral injunction at the core of industry, and failure punished by the threat of business extinction, it is unsurprising that many smaller eastern pharmaceutical companies will resort to expanding their business by going online and managing a longer reach of potential customers. As financial pressures intensify, ethical restraints for a range of actors associated with the pharmaceutical industry wilt under the strain of corrosive forces that are imposed on them by the neoliberal economy's pathogenic core (Hall 2012).

To fully understand the trade we have therefore positioned our analysis in a critical discussion of late-modern capitalist dynamics and processes of accumulation. The online trade in illicit medicines does not exist in a vacuum, but in many ways depends upon overarching processes of neoliberal globalisation, which include the current forms of pharmacy service found throughout the globe, wider national and local healthcare provisions and the general cultural, economic and technological environments that constitute and reproduce the overall neoliberal context (Mossialos et al. 2004). Our research has focused on the broad contexts of an interconnected global economy administered by deregulatory neoliberal politics, an attendant culture lacking 'symbolic efficiency' (Dean 2009; Winlow and Hall 2012) and thus reinforcing hyper-individualism, and an increasingly sophisticated and accessible technology and communications infrastructure. These contexts provide the conditions that are allowing a criminal market with a long history of gradual growth to now grow at a vastly accelerated rate. The online trade in illicit medicines is just one example of the way in which the ideological pursuit of profit in healthcare in both legitimate and illegitimate industries inflicts harm on the public. As a mutating 'shadow-market' (Hall and Winlow 2015) growing at an unprecedented rate in the context of a neoliberal capitalist system in a state of permanent economic and political crisis, these harms are likely to continue.

BIBLIOGRAPHY

Ahmed, T. (2009) 'Pharma Companies Rush to China'. *Pharma Deals Review*, 12, 126.

Albers-Miller, N.D. (1999) 'Consumer Misbehaviour: Why People Buy Illicit Goods'. *Journal of Consumer Marketing*, 16(3), 273–287.

Aldridge, J. and Décary-Hétu, D. (2014) 'Not an 'Ebay for Drugs': The Cryptomarket "Silk Road" as a Paradigm Shifting Criminal Innovation'. *Social Science Research Network*. Retrieved 8/4/16, from http://papers.ssrn.com/sol3/papers.cfm?abstract_id=2436643.

Anaman, P. (2014) 'Mapping Out Organised Crime Networks, Patterns and Trends'. Presentation at INTERPOL, Lyon, France, March 14.

Angop. (2013) 'Over 100 Tonnes of Illicit Medicines Seized in Southern Africa'. *Agencia Angola Press*. Retrieved 8/4/16, from http://www.portalangop.co.ao/angola/en_us/noticias/africa/2013/9/41/Over-100-tonnes-illicit-medicines-seized-Southern-Africa,dd68cbd6-7b7a-48fb-b129-3ccc44961ea8.html.

Antonopoulos, G.A. and Hall, S. (2014) 'The Death of the Legitimate Merchant?'. In van Duyne, P.C., Harvey, J., Antonopoulos, G.A., Maljevic, A., Markovska, A. and von Lampe, J. (eds) *Corruption, Greed and Crime Money*. 313–336. Nijmegen: Wolf Legal Publishers.

Antonopoulos, G.A. and Hall. A. (2016) 'Gain With No Pain': Anabolic-Androgenic Steroids Trafficking in the UK'. *European Journal of Criminology*, doi:10.1177/1477370816633261.

Antonopoulos, G.A. and Papanicolaou, G. (2014) *Unlicensed Capitalism, Greek Style: Illegal Markets and 'Organised Crime in Greece*. Nijmegen: Wolf Legal Publishers.

© The Author(s) 2016
A. Hall, G.A. Antonopoulos, *Fake Meds Online*,
DOI 10.1057/978-1-137-57088-8

ASMAG. (2012) 'Threats in Pharmaceutical Supply Chain'. *ASMAG,* April 30. Retrieved 30/04/12, from www.asmag.com.

Augé, M. (1995) *Non-Places: Introduction to an Anthropology of Supermodernity.* London: Verso.

Ball, J. (2013) 'Silk Road: The Online Drug Marketplace that Officials Seem Powerless to Stop', *The Guardian,* March 22. Retrieved 22/03/13, from http://www.theguardian.co.uk.

Banyai, M. and Glover, T.D. (2012) 'Evaluating Research Methods on Travel Blogs'. *Journal of Travel Research,* 51(3), 267–277.

Bate, R. (2008) *Making a Killing: The Deadly Implications of the Counterfeit Drug Trade.* Washington: AEI Press.

Bauman, Z. (1992) *Intimations of Postmodernity.* London: Routledge.

BBC Online. (1999) *UK's First Online Pharmacy Opens.* Retrieved 25/10/13, from http://news.bbc.co.uk/1/hi/health/537928.stm.

BBC Online. (2004) *Viagra Spam Fills Mail Inboxes.* Retrieved 27/9/14, from http://news.bbc.co.uk/1/hi/technology/3362489.stm.

BBC Online. (2008) *Online Drug Shopping 'Widespread'.* Retrieved 25/8/13, from http://news.bbc.co.uk/1/hi/health/7179653.stm.

BBC Online. (2011) *Free Movement of Prescription Drugs Hampers Regulation.* Retrieved 28/6/14, from http://www.bbc.co.uk/news/uk-northern-ireland-13938961.

Beckford, M. (2012) *'Alarming' Abuse of Prescription Drugs by Women, UN Warns.* Retrieved 3/10/13, from http://www.telegraph.co.uk/health/women_shealth/9356816/Alarming-abuse-of-prescription-drugs-by-women-UN-warns.html.

Beer, D. (2013) *Popular Culture and New Media: The Politics of Circulation.* London: Palgrave.

Beer, D. and Burrows, R. (2007) 'Sociology and, of and in Web 2.0: Some Initial Considerations'. *Sociological Research Online,* 12(5). Retrieved 20/9/13, from http://www.socresonline.org.uk/12/5/17.html.

Beer, D. and Burrows, R. (2010) 'An Introduction'. *Journal of Consumer Culture,* 10 (1), 3–12.

Bennett, T.H., Holloway, K., Brookman, F., Parry, O. and Gorden, C. (2013) 'Explaining Prescription Drug Misuse Among Students in a Widening Access University: The Role of Techniques of Neutralisation'. *Drugs: Education, Prevention and Policy,* 21(3): 448–455.

Bequai, A. (2001) 'Organised Crime Goes Cyber', *Computers and Security,* 20, 475–478.

Bickart, B. and Schindler, R.M. (2001) 'Internet Forums as Influential Sources of Consumer Information'. *Journal of interactive marketing,* 15(3), 31–40.

Bird, R.C. (2008) 'Counterfeit Drugs: A Global Consumer Perspective'. *Wake Forest Intellectual Property Law Journal,* 8(3), 387–406.

Blank, G. (2013) 'More of Us are Online, but We Feel Pretty Meh About It'. *The Conversation,* Retrieved 3/1013, from https://theconversation.com/more-of-us-are-online-but-we-feel-pretty-meh-about-it-18806.

Bogadich, W. (2007) 'Counterfeit Drugs' Path Eased by Free Trade Zones'. *New York Times.* Retrieved 3/12/13, from http://www.nytimes.com/2007/12/17/world/middleeast/17freezone.html?pagewanted=1&_r=1.

Boseley, S. (2008) 'Warning Over Fake Drugs on the Internet'. *The Guardian Online.* Retrieved 11/9/13, from http://www.guardian.co.uk/science/2008/jan/11/drugs.health.

Braithwaite, J. (1984) *Corporate Crime in the Pharmaceutical Industry.* London: Keegan Paul.

Brijnath, B. (2012) 'Pills, Pluralism, Risk, and Citizenship: Theorising E-Pharmacies'. *BioSocieties,* doi: 10.1057/biosoc.2012.11.

Bronshtein, D.M. (2008) 'Counterfeit Pharmaceuticals in China: Could Changes Bring Stronger Protection for Intellectual Property Rights and Human Health?'. *Pacific Rim Law and Policy Journal,* 17(2), 439–466.

Burke, D. (2014) 'Pangea Choke Points: Website Takedowns and Following the Money'. Presentation at INTEPOL, Lyon, France, March 13.

Butler, S.F., Venuti, S.W., Benoit, C., Beaulaurier, R.L., Houle, B. and Katz, N. (2007) 'Internet Surveillance, Content Analysis and Monitoring of Product-Specific Internet Prescription Opioid Abuse-Related Postings'. *Clinical Journal of Pain,* 23 (7), 619–628.

Byrne, M.D. (2012) 'Social Media and the Web 2.0 for the Paranaesthesia Nurse'. *Journal of the Paranaesthesia Nursing,* 27(5), 352–356.

Cassidy, N. (2012) 'Patients Struggle to Buy Drugs in Cash-Strapped Greece'. *BBC News Online.* Retrieved 7/6/14, from http://www.bbc.co.uk/news/business-18423966.

Castells, M. (2001) *The Internet Galaxy: Reflections on the Internet, Business and Society.* Oxford: Oxford University Press.

Castells, M. (2010) *End of Millennium: The Information Age: Economy, Society, and Culture Volume III.* London: Wiley-Blackwell.

Catterall, M. and Maclaran, P. (2002) 'Researching Consumers in Virtual Worlds: A Cyberspace Odyssey'. *Journal of Consumer Behaviour,* 1 (3), 228–237.

Cernea, M.V. and Uszkai, R. (2012) 'The Clash Between Global Justice and Pharmaceutical Patents: A Critical Analysis'. *Public Reason,* 4(1–2), 220–221.

Chan, S.P. (2013) *Viagra Maker Pfizer Faces Competition from Generic Rivals as Patent Expires.* Retrieved 3/12/13, from http://www.telegraph.co.uk/finance/newsbysector/pharmaceuticalsandchemicals/10095251/Viagra-maker-Pfizer-faces-competition-from-generic-rivals-as-patent-expires.html.

Chatwin, C. and Potter, G. (2014) 'Blurred Boundaries: The Artificial Distinction Between "Use" and "Supply" in the U.K. Cannabis Market'. *Contemporary Drug Problems,* 41(4), 536–550.

Chaudry, P. and Zimmerman, A. (2009) *The Economics of Counterfeit Trade: Governments, Consumers, Pirates and Intellectual Property Rights.* Berlin: Springer-Verlag.

China Pharmaceutical and Biotechnology Review. (2010) 'Drug Thugs: Counterfeit Pharmaceuticals'. *China Pharmaceutical and Biotechnology Review*, 40, 8–11.

China Pharmaceutical and Biotechnology Review. (2013a) 'CPB Weekly Round Up'. *China Pharmaceutical and Biotechnology Review*, October 16.

China Pharmaceutical and Biotechnology Review. (2013b) 'CPB Weekly Round Up'. *China Pharmaceutical and Biotechnology Review*, July 31.

Chowdhury, P. (2010) *An Overview of the Pharmaceutical Sector in Bangladesh.* Dhaka: BRAC.

Christin, N. (2012) *Travelling the Silk Road: A Measurement Analysis of a Large Anonymous Online Marketplace.* Carnegie Mellon INI/CyLab Working Paper. Pittsburgh, PA: Carnegie Mellon INI/CyLab.

CIPHP. (2007) *Pharmaceutical Distribution Systems in India.* Working paper 1a. Edinburgh: CIPHP.

Clark, E. (2008) *Counterfeit Medicines: The Pills that Kill.* Retrieved 3/12/13, from http://www.telegraph.co.uk/health/3354135/Counterfeit-medicines-the-pills-that-kill.html.

Cordell, V.V., Wongtada, N. and Kieschnick, R.L. (1996) 'Counterfeit Purchase Intentions'. *Journal of Business Research*, 35, 41–53.

Coscia, M. and Rios, V. (2012) 'Where Do Criminals Operate? Using Google to Track Mexican Drug Trafficking Organisations'. Harvard University. Retrieved 5/12/13, from: http://www.gov.harvard.edu/files/CosciaRios_GoogleForCriminals.pdf.

Davey, Z., Schifano, F., Corazza, O. and Deluca, P. (2012) 'e-Psychonauts: Conducting Research in Online Drug Forum Communities'. *Journal of Mental Health*, 21, 386–394.

Dean, J. (2005) 'Communicative Capitalism: Circulation and the Foreclosure of Politics'. *Cultural Politics*, 1(1), 51–74.

Dean, J. (2009) *Democracy and Other Neoliberal Fantasises: Communicative Capitalism and Left Politics.* Durham: Duke University Press.

DeKieffer, D.E. (2006) 'The Internet and the Globalization of Counterfeit Drugs'. *Journal of Pharmacy Practice*, 19, 171–177.

Dellarocas, C. (2006) 'Strategic Manipulation of Internet Opinion Forums: Implications for Consumers and Firms'. *Management science*, 52(10), 1577–1593.

Deloitte. (2011) *The Next Phase: Opportunities in China's Pharmaceutical Market.* London: Deloitte.

Di Nicola, A., Martini, E. and Baratto, G. (2015) *Trick or Treat(ment)? Guidelines for Safe Online Purchases of Medicinal Products in the EU.* Trento:

eCrime – University of Trento. Retrieved 7/4/16, from http://fakecare.
com/images/pdf/FAKECARE-Guidelines_for_Customers.pdf.

Di Nicola, A., Martini, E. and Baratto, G. (2016) *FAKECARE: Developing Expertise Against the Online Trade of Fake Medicines by Producing and Disseminating Knowledge, Counterstrategies and Tools Across the EU.* eCrime Research Reports No.2. Trento: eCrime – University of Trento.

Dixon-Fyle, S. and Kowallik, T. (2010) *Engaging Consumers to Manage Health Care Demand.* London: McKinsey.

Dobson, M. (2013) *The Story of Medicine.* London: Quercus.

Dorn, N., Murji, K. and South, N. (1992) *Traffickers.* London: Routledge.

EAEPC. (2013) *How Does it Work?.* Retrieved 6/11/13, from http://eaepc.
chiemgau-net.de/en/how-does-it-work/.

Edwards, L., Klein, B., Lee, D., Moss, G. and Philip, F. (2012) Framing the Consumer: Copyright Regulation and the Public. *Convergence*, 19(9). doi:10.1177/1354856512456788.

EFPIA. (2012) *The Pharmaceutical Industry in Figures.* Brussels: EFPIA.

Ehrenreich, B., Dowie, M. and Minkin, S. (1980) 'Dangerous Contraceptives=Big Business'. *Spare Rib*, Issue 90, 6–7.

Einhorn, B., Loo, D. and Khan, N. (2011) 'Bashing Big Pharma in China'. *Bloomberg Businessweek.* Retrieved 10/11/11, from www.businessweek.com.

Ellis, S. (2009) 'West Africa's International Drug Trade'. *African Affairs*, 108(431), 2009: 171–196.

European Parliament. (2011) *Differences in Costs of and Access to Pharmaceutical Products in the EU.* Brussels: European Parliament.

Exantas. (2013) 'Zoi Copyright', *NetTV,* April 17.

Feng, H. (2013) 'Jack of All Things Internet'. *China Daily,* May 17–23, p. 9.

Fielding, N., Lee, R M. and Blank, G. (eds.) (2008) *Online Research Methods.* London: Sage.

Filipkowski, W. (2004) 'Internet as an Illegal Market Place'. Paper presented at the 6th Cross-Border Crime Colloquium, Berlin, Germany, October.

Fincoeur, B., van de Ven, K. and Mulrooney, K.J.D. (2014) 'The Symbiotic Evolution of Anti-Doping and Supply Chains of Doping Substances'. *Trends in Organised Crime*, doi: 10.1007/s12117-014-9235-7.

Finlay, B.D. (2011) *Counterfeit Drugs and National Security.* Washington, D.C.: The Stimson Centre.

First World Pharma. (2012) 'China – Big Pharma Investment Grows'. *First World Pharma.* Retrieved 23/09/12, from www.firstworldpharma.com.

Fishwick, L., Sillence, E., Briggs, P. and Harris, P. (2008). 'Women's Identity and Consumption of Health Discourse on the Internet'. In Caudwell, J., Redhead, S. and Tomlinson, A. eds. *Relocating the Leisure Society: Media, Consumption and Spaces.* Brighton: LSA.

Fisse, B. and Braithwaite, J. (1993) *Corporations, Crime and Accountability.* Cambridge: Cambridge University Press.

Flower, R. (2004) 'Lifestyle Drugs: Pharmacology and the Social Agenda'. *Trends in Pharmacological Sciences,* 25 (4), 182–185.

Ford, N. (2013) 'Locals Want Bigger Share of $40bn Industry'. *African Business,* No.397 (May), 16–29.

Fotiou, F., Aravid, S., Wang, P.P. and Nerapusee, O. (2009) 'Impact of Illegal Trade on the Quality of Epoetin Alfa in Thailand'. *Clinical Therapy,* 31(2), 336–346.

Fox, N.J., O'Rourke, A. and Ward, K.J. (2005a) *Consumerism, Information and Drug Prescribing Governance* (End of award report), Economic and Social Research Council, UK.

Fox, N.J., Ward, K.J. and O'Rourke, A. (2005b) 'The 'Expert Patient': Empowerment or Medical Dominance? The Case of Weight Loss and the Internet'. *Social Science and Medicine,* 60 (6): 1299–1309.

Fox, N.J., Ward, K.J. and O'Rourke, A. (2005c) 'Pro-Anorexia, Weight-Loss Drugs and the Internet: An 'Anti-Recovery' Explanatory Model of Anorexia'. *Sociology of Health & Illness,* 27 (7), 944–971.

Fox, N.J., Ward, K.J. and O'Rourke, A. (2005d) 'The Birth of the E-Clinic. Continuity or Transformation in the UK Governance of Pharmaceutical Consumption?'. *Social Science & Medicine,* 61 (17), 1474–54.

Fox N.J. and Ward K.J. (2006) 'Health Identities: From Expert Patient to Resisting Consumer'. *Health,* 10 (4), 461–479.

Fox N.J. and Ward K.J. (2008) 'What Are Health Identities and How May We Study Them?'. *Sociology of Health and Illness,* 30 (7), 1007–1021.

Foxton, W. (2012) *Web Traffic: The Internet is Dramatically Changing the Way Drug Dealers Do Business.* Retrieved 10/9/13, from http://www.kernelmag.com/features/report/2805/how-the-internet-is-changing-the-drug-trade/.

Garde, D. (2013) 'Outsourcing in China: Big Pharma Wants Partners'. *FierceCRO.* Retrieved 07/04/16, from www.fierceco.com.

Geertz, C. (1973) *The Interpretation of Cultures.* New York: Basic Books.

Gilbert, D., Walley, T. and New, B. (2000) 'Lifestyle Medicines'. *British Medical Journal,* 321, 1341–1344.

Goldacre, B. (2012) *Bad Pharma.* London: Fourth Estate.

GQ. (2013) 'Business Special'. *GQ,* February, pp. 186–189.

Gregory, J. (2013) *Counterfeits Peddler Fined £5.6m After UK's 'Most Serious' Supply Chain Breach.* Retrieved 26/11/13, from http://www.chemistand-druggist.co.uk/news-content/-/article_display_list/15947486/counterfeits-peddler-fined-5-6m-after-uk-s-most-serious-supply-chain-breach.

Groves, K. (2014) 'Payment Systems and Illegal Online Pharmacies'. Presentation at INTERPOL, Lyon, France, March 13.

Guardian Online. (2013) *Warning of NHS Mental Health Crisis.* Retrieved 16 October, 2013, from http://www.theguardian.com/society/2013/oct/16/warning-crisis-nhs-mental-health.

Guarnieri, F. and Przyswa, E. (2013) 'Counterfeiting and Cybercrime: Stakes and Challenges'. *The Information Society: An International Journal,* 29(4), 219–226.

Gupta, H., Kumar, S., Roy, S.K. and Gaud, S.R. (2010) 'Patent Protection Strategies'. *Journal of Pharmacy and Bio-Allied Sciences,* 2(1), 2–7.

Halford, S., Pope, C. and Weal, M.J. (2012) 'Digital Futures? Sociological Challenges and Opportunities in the Emergent Semantic Web'. *Sociology,* 47, (1), 173–189.

Hall, S. (2012) *Theorising Crime and Deviance.* London: Sage.

Hall, A. and Antonopoulos, G.A. (2015) 'License to Pill: Illegal Entrepreneurs' Tactics in the Online Trade of Medicines'. In van Duyne, P.C., Maljevic, A., Antonopoulos, G.A., Harvey, J. and von Lampe, K. (eds) *The Relativity of Wrongdoing: Corruption, Organised Crime, Fraud and Money Laundering in Perspective.* (pp. 229–252) Nijmegen: Wolf Legal Publisher.

Hall, A and Antonopoulos, G.A. (2016a) *Developing an In-Depth Knowledge of the Online Trade of Falsified Medicinal Products in the United Kingdom.* Trento: eCrime – University of Trento.

Hall, A and Antonopoulos, G.A. (2016b) 'Coke on Tick: Exploring the Cocaine Market in the UK through the Lens of Financial Management'. *Journal of Financial Crime.* Forthcoming.

Hall, S and Winlow, S. (2015) *Revitalizing Criminological Theory. Towards a New Ultra-Realism.* Oxon: Routledge.

Hall, S., Winlow, S. and Ancrum, C. (2008) *Criminal Identities and Consumer Culture.* Cullompton: Willan.

Hall, A., Antonopoulos, G.A., Di Nicola, A., Martini, E. and Baratto, G. (2015) *Search and Stop: Guidelines toTtackle the Online Trade of Falsified Medicinal Products.* Trento: eCrime – University of Trento. Retrieved 7/4/16, from http://fakecare.com/images/pdf/FAKECARE-Guidelines_for_LEAs.pdf.

Hansson, L., Wrangmo, A. and Solberg Søilen, K. (2013) 'Optimal Ways for Companies to Use Facebook as a Marketing Channel'. *Journal of Information, Communication and Ethics in Society,* 11(2), 112–126.

Harvey, D. (2005) *A Brief History of Neoliberalism.* Oxford: Oxford University Press.

Harvey, N. (2012) 'The Cost of Living: How Drug Patents are Killing the Poor'. *The New Internationalist,* No.457, 16–18.

Haugen, H, Ø. (2011) 'Chinese Exports to Africa: Competition, Complementarity and Cooperation between Micro-Level Actors'. *Forum for Development Studies,* 38(2), 157–176.

Hayward, K. (2012) 'Using Cultural Geography to Think Critically About Space and Crime'. In Hall, S. and Winlow, S. (eds) *New Directions in Criminological Theory* (pp. 123–144). London: Routledge.

He, W., Zha, S. and Li, L. (2013) 'Social Media Competitive Analysis and Text Mining'. *International Journal of Information Management*, 33, 464–472.

Hemphill, C.S. and Sampat, B.N. (2012) 'Evergreening, Patent Challenges and Effective Market Life in Pharmaceuticals'. *Journal of Health Economics*, 31, 327–339.

Hetzer, W. (2002) 'Godfathers and Pirates: Counterfeiting and Organized Crime'. *European Journal of Crime, Criminal Law and Criminal Justice*, 10 (4), 303–320.

Hine, C. (2000) *Virtual Ethnography*. London: Sage.

Hine, C. (2008) 'Virtual Ethnography: Modes, Varieties, Affordances'. In Fielding, N., Lee, R.M. and Blank, G. (eds.) *Online Research Methods* (pp. 257–270). London: Sage.

Hobbs, D. (1995) *Bad Business*. Oxford: Oxford University Press.

Hobbs, D. (1997) 'Professional Crime: Change, Continuity and the Enduring Myth of the Underworld'. *Sociology*, 31, 57–72.

Hobbs, D. (1998) 'Going Down the Glocal: The Local Context of Organised Crime'. *Howard Journal of Criminal Justice*, 37(4), 407–422.

Hobbs, D. (2001) 'The Firm: Organisational Logic and Criminal Culture in a Shifting Terrain'. *British Journal of Criminology*, 41, 549–560.

Hobbs, D. (2013) *Lush Life*. Oxford: Oxford University Press.

Hobbs, D. and Antonopoulos, G.A. (2014) 'How to Research Organised Crime'. In Paoli, L. (ed.) *The Oxford Handbook of Organised Crime*. (pp. 96–117) New York: OUP.

Hoffer, L.D., Bobashev, G. and Morris, R.J. (2009) 'Researching a Local Heroin Market as a Complex Adaptive System'. *American Journal of Community Psychology*, 44, 273–286.

Hofmann, J. (2013) 'The Trouble With Emerging Pharma'. *Investors Chronicle*, August 2–8, 52–53.

Holloway, K. and Bennett, T.H. (2012) 'Prescription Drug Misuse Among University Staff and Students: A Survey of Motives, Nature and Extent'. *Drugs: Education, Prevention & Policy*, 19 (2), 137–144.

Holloway, K., Bennett, T.H., Parry, O. and Gorden, C. (2013) 'Misuse of Prescription Drugs on University Campuses: Options for Prevention'. *International Review of Law, Computers and Technology*, 27(3), 324–334.

Holt, T.J. and Copes, H. (2010) 'Transferring Subcultural Knowledge Online'. *Deviant Behaviour*, 31, 625–654.

Huang, L., Yung, C.-Y., Yang, E. (2011) 'How do Travel Agencies Obtain a Competitive Advantage'. *Journal of Vacation Marketing*, 17(2), 139–149.

Hudson, M. (2015) *Killing the Host: How Financial Parasites and Debt Destroy the Global Economy*. New York: Avalon.

Huff, E.A. (2012) 'China Bypasses Big Pharma Patents, Authorises Low-Cost Generic Drug Manufacturing'. *Natural News.* Retrieved 27/06/2012, from www.naturalnews.com.

IRACM. (2013) *Counterfeit Medicines and Criminal Organisations.* Paris: IRACM.

Ivanitskaya, L., Brookins-Fisher, J., O Boyle, I., Vibbert, D., Erofeev, D. and Fulton, L. (2010) 'Dirt Cheap and Without Prescription: How Susceptible Are Young US Consumers to Purchasing Drugs from Rogue Internet Pharmacies?'. *Journal Medical Internet Research,* 12 (2), doi: 10.2196/jmir.1520.

Jack, A. (2016) 'Can Anyone Stop the Illegal Sale of Medicines Online?'. *British Medical Journal,* 352. Retrieved 7/4/2016, from http://www.bmj.com/content/352/bmj.i1317?etoc.

Jackson, G., Patel, S. and Khan, S. (2012) 'Assessing the Problem of Counterfeit Medications in the United Kingdom'. *International Journal of Clinical Practice,* 66 (3), 241–250.

Janetzko, D. (2008) 'Nonreactive Data Collection on the Internet'. In Fielding, N., Lee, R.M. and Blank, G. (eds.) *Online Research Methods* (pp. 161–174) London: Sage.

JDSU. (2010) *Pharmaceutical Counterfeiting, Tampering, and Diversion: Solutions for Addressing a Growing Threat.* Los Angeles, Ca: JDSU.

Jessop, B. (2004) 'Critical Semiotic Analysis and Cultural Political Economy'. *Critical Discourse Studies,* 1(2), pp 159–174.

Jewkes, Y. (2011) 'The Media and Criminological Research'. In Davies, P., Francis, P. and Jupp, V. (eds) *Doing Criminological Research* (pp. 245–261). London: Sage.

Jewkes, Y. and Yar, M. (eds.) (2010) *Handbook of Internet Crime.* Collumpton: Willan.

Jopson, B. (2013) 'US Shoppers Spurn Retail Therapy as Malls Struggle'. *Financial Times,* February 9–10, p. 5.

Jürgens, P., Jungherr, A. and Schoen, H. (2011) 'Small Worlds with a Difference'. Presentation at *WebSci 2011,* Koblenz, Germany, June 14–17.

Kangaspunta, K. and Musumeci, M. (2014) 'Trafficking in Counterfeit Goods'. In Reichel, P. and Albanese, J. (eds.) *Handbook of Transnational Crime and Justice.* 2nd Edition. London: Sage.

Kaplan, A.M. and Haenlein, M. (2010) 'Users of the World Unite! The Challenges and Opportunities of Social Media'. *Business Horizons,* 53, 59–68.

Kean, J. (2012) *Anabolic steroids.* Unpublished MSc Criminology Dissertation, Middlesbrough: Teesside University.

Keeling, N. (2014) 'Bitter Pill as Viagra Fraudster is Jailed'. *Manchester Evening News,* October 3, p5.

Kennedy, J.P. and Wilson, J.M. (2015) Charting the Course: The Roles and Responsibilities of Ocean-Going Transportation Intermediaries in the Distribution of Counterfeit Goods. Center for Anti-Counterfeiting and

Product Protection Paper Series. Retrieved 8/4/16, from http://a-capp.msu.edu/sites/default/files/Intermediary%20Liability_FINAL.pdf.

Kimes, M. (2010) 'Big Pharma's Challenge: Figuring Out China'. *CNN*, September 23.

Klein, J.D. and Wilson K.M. (2003) 'Delivering Quality Care: Adolescent's Discussion of Health Risks with Their Providers'. *Journal of Adolescent Health*, 30 (3), 190–195.

Koenraadt, R. (2012) 'Blue Pills on the Black Market'. *CIROC Newsletter*, 10(12), 4–5.

Kovacs Burns, K. and Morrice, D. (2004) ''Cross-Border Internet Pharmacies: What are the Issues? What is Less Obvious?', *Journal of Pharmaceutical Marketing and Management*, 16(3), 29–52.

KPMG. (2012) *An Overview of Risk and Disclosure in the Global Pharmaceutical and Life Sciences Industry*. Retrieved 2/1/14, from http://www.kpmg.com/global/en/issuesandinsights/articlespublications/pages/risk-and-disclosure-in-the-global-pharmaceutical-industry.aspx.

Krebs on Security. (2011) 'SpamIt, Glavmed Pharmacy Networks Exposed', *KrebsOnSecurity*, February, 2011. Retrieved 8/4/16, from https://krebsonsecurity.com/2011/02/spamit-glavmed-pharmacy-networks-exposed/.

Laing, B.A. (2005) 'Parallel Trade in Pharmaceuticals: Injecting the Counterfeit Element into the Public Health'. *NC Journal of International Law and Commercial Regulation*, 31(4), 847–900.

Laing, B.A. and Mackey, T. (2009) 'Searching for Safety: Addressing Search Engine, Website, and Provider Accountability for Illicit Online Drug Sales'. *American Journal of Law and Medicines*, 35, 125–184.

Laing, B. and Mackey, T.K. (2011) 'Prevalence and Global Health Implications of Social Media in Direct-to-Consumer Drug Advertising'. *Journal of Medical Internet Research*, 13(3). Retrieved 7/4/16, from http://www.ncbi.nlm.nih.gov/pmc/articles/PMC3222189/.

Lavorgna, A. (2015) 'The Online Trade in Counterfeit Pharmaceuticals'. *European Journal of Criminology*, 12(2), 226–241.

Law, J. (2006) *Big Pharma: How the World's Biggest Companies Control Illness*. London: Constable.

Levi, M. (2001) 'Between the Risk and the Reality Falls the Shadow: Evidence and Urban Legends in Computer Fraud'. In Wall, D. (ed.) *Crime and the Internet*. (pp. 44–58) Abingdon: Routledge.

Levi, M. (2002) 'Breaking the Economic Power of Organised Crime Groups'. Paper presented at the CIROC (Centre for Information and Research on Organised Crime) seminar. Amsterdam, The Netherlands, 16th October.

Levi, M. (2015) 'Qualitative Research on Elite Frauds, Ordinary Frauds and Organised Crime'. In Miller, M. and Copes, H. (eds.) *Handbook of Qualitative Criminology*. (pp. 215–235) New York: Routledge.

Levi, M. and Naylor, R.T. (2000) 'Organised Crime, the Organisation of Crime, and the Organisation of Business'. DTI Crime Foresight Panel Essay. Retrieved 7/4/16, from http://www.cf.ac.uk/socsi/resources/levi-orgcrime.pdf.

Lingel, J. (2012) 'Ethics and Dilemmas of Online Ethnography'. Presentation at *CHI 2012*, Austin, Texas, May 5–10.

Littlejohn, C., Baldacchino, A., Schifano, F. and Deluca, P. (2005) 'Internet Pharmacies and Online Prescription Drug Sales: A Cross-Sectional Study'. *Drugs: Education, Prevention & Policy*, 12(1), 75–80.

Mackenzie, S. (2012) 'Fakes'. In Brookman, F., Maguire, M., Pierpoint, H. and Bennett, T. (eds) *Handbook on Crime*. (pp. 120–136). Cullompton: Willan.

Mallick, T. (2013) 'The Artists of Innovation'. *The New Economy*, Spring, 1–15.

Management Today. (2013) 'The Future of Payments is Virtual'. *Management Today*, January, 50–51.

Martin, J. (2014) Drugs on the Dark Net: How Cryptomarkets Are Transforming the Global Trade in Illicit Drugs. Basingstoke: Palgrave Macmillan.

Maskus, K.E. (2002) *Parallel Imports in Pharmaceuticals: Implications for Competition and Prices in Developing Counties*. Final report to the World Intellectual Property Organisation.

McCusker, R. (2006) 'Transnational Organised Cyber-Crime: Distinguishing Threat from Reality'. *Crime, Law and Social Change*, 46, 257–273.

McDonald, M. and Wearing, S. (2013) *Social Psychology and Theories of Consumer Culture: A Political Economy Perspective*. London: Routledge.

McKee, R. (2013) 'Ethical Issues in Using Social Media for Health and Health Care Purposes'. *Health Policy*, 110, 298–301.

McQuade, S. (2011) 'Technology-Enabled Crime, Policing and Security'. *The Journal of Technology Studies*, 32(1), 1–9.

Medical Daily. 'Illegal Online Pharmacies Exploiting the Web'. *Medical Daily*, August 17, 2011.

MHRA. (2013) *Press Release: MHRA Nets UK Record £12.2 Million Haul of Counterfeit and Unlicensed Medicines*. Retrieved 15/7/13, from http://www.mhra.gov.uk/NewsCentre/Pressreleases/CON287024.

Miah, A. and Rich, E. (2008) *The Medicalization of Cyberspace*. London: Routledge.

Monnet, B. and Véry, P. (2010) Les noveaux pirates de l'entreprise, Mafias et terrorisme. Paris: CNRS editions.

Moore, W. (2000) 'House Call: No Appointments, No Waiting, Speedy Diagnosis and Prescription – Online Doctors Are Flourishing. But Are They Safe'. *Guardian Online*. Retrieved 25/8/13, from http://www.guardian.co.uk/theobserver/2000/jun/04/life1.lifemagazine6?INTCMP=SRCH.

Moore, R. (2007) 'The Role of Computer Forensics in Criminal Investigations'. In Jewkes, Y. (ed.) *Crime Online*. (pp. 81–94). Cullompton: Willan.

Morgan, O. (2008) 'Parallel Trade in Drugs Puts EU Patients at Risk'. *The Guardian Online*. Retrieved 13/9/13, from http://www.theguardian.com/business/2008/jun/29/pharmaceuticals.

Morris, J. and Stevens, P. (2006) *Countefeit Medicines in Less Developed Countries: Problems and Solutions*. London: International Policy Network.

Mossialos, E., Mrazek, M. and Walley, T. (eds) (2004) *Regulating Pharmaceuticals in Europe: Striving for Efficiency, Equity and Quality*. Maidenhead: Open University Press.

Moyle, L. and Coomber, R. (2015) 'Earning A Score: An Exploration of the Nature and Roles of Heroin and Crack Cocaine 'User-Dealers'. *The British Journal of Criminology*, doi: 10.1093/bjc/azu087.

Moynihan, R., Heath, I. and Henry, D. (2002) 'Selling Sickness: The Pharmaceutical Industry and Disease Mongering'. *British Medical Journal*, 324, 886–891.

Naylor, R.T. (2000) *Economic and Organised Crime: Challenges for Criminal Justice*. Ottawa: Research and Statistics Division.

Neate, R. and Farrell, S. (2014) 'Pfizer's Attempt on AstraZeneca Leaves a Bitter Taste in Sandwich'. *The Observer*, May 4, 40–41.

Neveling, P. (2015) 'Free Trade Zones, Export Processing Zones, Special Economic Zones and Global Imperial Formations 200 Bce to 2015 Ce'. In Ness, I. and Cope, Z. (eds.) *The Palgrave Encyclopedia of Imperialism and Anti-Imperialism* (pp. 1007–16). Basingstoke: Palgrave Macmillan.

News24/7. (2013) 'Lack of Pharmaceuticals: 147 Types of Medicines Disappeared'. *News24/7*. Retrieved 07/04/16, from www.news247.gr.

Nielsen, S. and Barratt, M.J. (2009) 'Prescription Drug Misuse: Is Technology Friend or Foe?'. *Drug and Alcohol Review*, 28 (1), 81–6.

Nordstrom, C. (2007) *Global Outlaws: Crime, Money, and Power in the Contemporary World*. Los Angeles, CA: University of California Press.

ONS. (2013) 'Internet Access – Households and Individuals, 2013'. *Office for National Statistics*, Retrieved 25/9/14, from http://www.ons.gov.uk/ons/rel/rdit2/internet-access---households-and-individuals/2013/stb-ia-2013.html.

Orizio, G., Schulz, P., Domenighini, S., Caimi, L., Rosati, C., Rubinelli, S and Gelatti, U. (2009) 'Cyberdrugs: A Cross-Sectional Study of Online Pharmacies Characteristics'. *European Journal of Public Health*, 19(4), 375–377.

Palmer, E. (2013) 'China Cooperating with Big Pharma to Fight Counterfeiting'. *Fierce Pharma Manufacturing*, January 22, p. 1.

Paoli, L. and Donati, A. (2014) *The Sports Doping Market*. New York: Spinger.

Passas, N. (1999) 'Globalisation, Criminogenic Asymmetries, and Economic Crime'. *European Journal of Law Reform*, 1, 399–423.

Passas, N. (2005) 'Lawful but Awful: Legal Corporate Crimes'. *Journal of Socio-Economics*, 34, 771–786.

Pearson, G. and Hobbs, D. (2001) *Middle Market Drug Distribution*. London: Home Office.

Permanent Forum on International Pharmaceutical Crime (PFIPC). (2014) *Investigators' Guide for the Conduct of Internet Investigations Concerning Illegal Internet Pharmacies*. Unpublished investigators' guide.

Podder, A., Foreman, J., Banerjee, S. and Ellen, P. (2011) 'Exploring the Robin Hood Effect: Moral Profiteering Motives for Purchasing Counterfeit Products'. *Journal of Business Research*. Retrieved 8/4/16, from http://papers.ssrn.com/sol3/papers.cfm?abstract_id=2135152.

Port Technology. (2015) *China-Kazakhstan's Massive Cargo Connection*. Retrieved 6/4/16, from https://www.porttechnology.org/news/china_kazakhstans_massive_cargo_connection.

Portes, A., Castells, M. and Benton, L.A. (eds.). (1991) *The Informal Economy: Studies in Advanced and Less Developed Countries*. Baltimore, MD: John Hopkins University Press.

Post, R.C., Eder, J., Maniscalco, S., Johnson-Bailey, D. and Bard, S. (2013) 'MyPlate is Now Reaching More Consumers Through Social Media', *Journal of the Academy of Nutrition and Dietetics*, 113(6), 754–755.

Power, M. (2013) *Drugs 2.0: The Web Revolution that is Changing How the World Gets High*. London: Portobello Books.

PSI. (2006) *Annual Situation Report, 2005*. Vienna: Pharmaceutical Security Institute.

Raine, C., Webb, D.J. and Maxwell, S.R.J. (2008) 'The Availability of Prescription Only Analgesics Purchased from the Internet in the UK'. *British Journal of Clinical Pharmacology*, 67(2), 250–254.

Reynolds, L., Attaran, A., Hervey, T. and McKee, M. (2012) 'Competition-Based Reform of the National Health Service in England: A One-Way Street'. *International Journal of Health Services*, 42(2), 213–217.

Ritzer, G. and Jurgenson, N. (2010) 'Production, Consumption, Prosumption: The Nature of Capitalism in the Age of the Digital 'Prosumer''. *Journal of Consumer Culture*, 10 (1), 13–36.

Rodham, K. and Gavin, J. (2006) 'The Ethics of Using the Internet to Gather Qualitative Research Data'. *Research Ethics Review*, 2 (3), 92–97.

Ruggiero, V. (2000) *Crime and Markets*. Oxford: Oxford University Press.

Ruggiero, V. (2003) 'Global Markets and Crime'. In Beare, M. (ed.) *Critical Reflections on Organised Crime, Money Laundering, and Corruption* (pp. 171–182). Toronto: University of Toronto Press.

Rutter, J. and Bryce, J. (2008) 'The Consumption of Counterfeit Goods: 'Here be Pirates?''. *Sociology*, 42, 1146.

Ryan, A. and Sancilio, F.D. (2013) 'Outsourcing Excellence in China and India'. *Pharma Manufacturing*. January 8. Retrieved 07/04/15, from www.pharma-manufacturing.com.

Saini, K., Saini, N. and Baldi, A. (2011) 'Impact of Anti-Counterfeiting Trade Agreement on Pharma Sector: A Global Perspective'. *Journal of Current Pharmaceutical Research*, 6(1), 4–10.

Sassatelli, R. (2007) *Consumer Culture: History, Theory and Politics*. London: Sage.

Sassen, S. (1998) *Globalisation and its Discontents: Essays on the New Mobility of People and Money*. New York: The New Press.

Sassen, S. (2007) *A Sociology of Globalization*. New York: W. W. Norton.

Satchwell, G. (2004) *A Sick Business: Counterfeit Medicines and Organised Crime*. The Stockholm Network.

Savona, E.U. and Mignone, M. (2004) 'The Fox and the Hunter': How IC Technologies Changes the Crime Race'. *European Journal on Criminal Policy and Research*, 10, 3–26.

Sayer, A. (1999) 'Long Live Postdisciplinary Studies! Sociology and the Curse of Disciplinary Parochialism/Imperialism'. Department of Sociology, Lancaster University. Retrieved 7/4/16, from http://www.lancaster.ac.uk/fass/resources/sociology-online-papers/papers/sayer-long-live-postdisciplinary-studies.pdf.

Schifano, F., Deluca, P., Baldacchino, A., Peltoniemi, T., Scherbaum, N. and Torrens, M. (2006) 'Drugs on the Web: The Psychonaut 2002 EU project'. *Progress in Neuro-psychopharmacology and Biological Psychiatry*, 30, 640–6.

Schmidt, M.M., Sharma, A., Schifano, F. and Feinmann, C. (2011) '"Legal Highs" on the Net—Evaluation of UK-Based Websites, Products and Product Information'. Forensic Science International, 206 (1–3), 92–97.

Schwalbe, M.L. & Wolkomir, M. (2003) 'Interviewing Men'. In Holstein J.A. & Gubrium J.F. (eds.) *Inside Interviewing: New Lenses, New Concerns.* (pp. 55–71) Thousand Oaks, CA: Sage.

Science Daily. (2011) 'Tracking Illegal Online Pharmacies: Evidence of Web Manipulation', *Science Daily*, August 12. Retrieved 8/4/16, from https://www.sciencedaily.com/releases/2011/08/110811151327.htm.

Shank, M. (2010) 'Specialty Drugmaker Sinobiopharma Takes on Big Pharma in China'. *Bloomberg*, November 12. Retrieved 07/04/2016, from www.bloomberg.com.

Shares. (2013) 'Healthy Gains'. *Shares*, May 16, pp 14–23.

Shaxson, N. (2011) *Treasure Islands: Uncovering the Damage of Offshore Banking and Tax Havens*. New York: St. Martin's Press.

Shover, N., Coffey, G.S. and Hobbs, D. (2003) 'Crime on the Line': Telemarketing and the Changing Nature of Professional Crime'. British Journal of Criminology, 43, 489–505.

Sillence, E. and Briggs, P. (2007). 'Examining the Role of the Internet in Health'. In Jonson, A.N., McKenna, K.Y.A., Postmes, T. and Reips, U.D. (eds.) *The Oxford Handbook of Internet Psychology*. Oxford: Oxford University Press, 347–359.

Singh Bansal, I., Sahu, D., Bakshi, G. and Singh, S. (2009) 'Evergreening – A Controversial Issue in Pharma Milieu'. *Journal of Intellectual Property Rights*, 14, 299–306.

Siva, N. (2010) *Tackling the Booming Trade in Counterfeit Drugs*. The Lancet. Retrieved 3 December, 2103, http://www.thelancet.com/journals/lancet/article/PIIS0140-6736(10)62118-6/fulltext.

Slevin, J. (2000) *The Internet and Society*. Cambridge: Polity Press

Smart, B. (2010) *Consumer Society: Critical Issues and Environmental Consequences*. London: Sage.

Smithers, R. (2013) *Surge in Purchases of Counterfeit Goods*. The Guardian. Retrieved 3/12/13, from http://www.theguardian.com/money/2013/oct/02/counterfeit-goods-surge-uk.

Soudijn, M.R.J. and Zegers, B.C.H. (2012) 'Cyber-Crime and Virtual Offender Convergence'. *Trends in Organised Crime*, 15(2/3), 111–129.

Southwick, N. (2013) *Counterfeit Drugs Kill 1 Million People Annually: Interpol*. 26/11/13, from http://www.insightcrime.org/news-briefs/counterfeit-drugs-kill-1-million-annually-interpol.

Spellwin, G. (2004) *The Secrets of Mail Order Steroid Success*. Retrieved 07/04/16, from www.elitefitness.com.

St. George, B.B.N., Emmanuel, J.R. and Middleton, K.L. (2004) 'Overseas-Based Online Pharmacies: A Source of Supply for Illicit Drug Users?'. *Medical Journal Australia*, 180, 118–119.

Su, C. and Holt, T.J. (2010) 'Cyber-Bullying in Chinese Web Forums: An Examination of Nature and Extent'. *International Journal of Cyber Criminology*, 4(1 and 2), 672–684.

Sugiura, L., Pope, C. and Webber, C. (2012) 'Buying Unlicensed Slimming Drugs from the Web: A Virtual Ethnography'. *Web Science Conference 2012*. Retrieved 8/4/16, from http://eprints.soton.ac.uk/340989/1/Web_sci_12_submission_FINAL.pdf.

Swami, V., Chamorro-Premuzic, T. and Furnham, A. (2009) 'Faking it: Personality and Individual Difference Predictors of Willingness to Buy Counterfeit Goods'. *Journal of Socio-Economics*, 38 (5), 820–825.

Swyngedouw, E. (2004) 'Globalisation or Glocalisation? Networks, Territories and Rescaling'. *Cambridge Review of International Affairs*, 17(1), 25–48.

The Economist. (2013a) Alibaba: The World's Greatest Bazaar. Retrieved 3/11/13, from http://www.economist.com/news/briefing/21573980-alibaba-trailblazing-chinese-internet-giant-will-soon-go-public-worlds-greatest-bazaar.

The Economist. (2013b) 'The Alibaba Phenomenon'. *The Economist*, March 23, p. 14 and 25–26.

The New York Times. (2012) 'Cough Syrup Suspected to Have Killed 33 in Pakistan'. *The New York Times*, December 29. Retrieved 07/04/16, from http://www.nytimes.com/2012/12/30/world/asia/cough-syrup-suspected-to-have-killed-33-in-pakistan.html?_r=0.

The Psychologist. (2013) 'NHS Developments'. *The Psychologist*, 26(2), p. 91.

Thomsen, S.R. (1998) 'Ethnomethodology and the Study of Online Communities: Exploring the Cyber Streets'. *Information Research*, 4 (1). Retrieved 07/04/16, from http://informationr.net/ir/4-1/paper50.html.

Toffler, A. (1980) *The Third Wave*. New York: William Morrow & Co.

Travers, R.L. (2012) 'Social Media in Dermatology: Moving to Web 2.0'. *Seminars in Cutaneous Medicine and Surgery*, 31(3), 168–172.

Treadwell, J. (2011) 'From the Car Boot to Booting it Up? eBay, Online Counterfeit Crime, and the Transformation of the Criminal Marketplace'. *Criminology and Criminal Justice*, 12(2), 175–191.

Truick, S. (2014) 'Identifying and Stopping Illicit Online Pharmacies'. Presentation at INTERPOL, Lyon, France, March 14.

Tse, E., Sun, S., Pan, P. and Ma, K. (2012) *Changing Landscape of China's Pharmaceutical Distribution Industry*. Hong Kong: BoozandCo.

UNODC. (2007) *Cocaine Trafficking in West Africa: The Threat to Stability and Development*. Retrieved 3/11/13, from http://www.unodc.org/documents/data-and-analysis/west_africa_cocaine_report_2007-12_en.pdf.

UNODC. (2010) *The Globalisation of Crime: A Transnational Organised Crime Threat Assessment*. Vienna: UNODC.

UNODC. (2015) *The Illicit Trafficking in Counterfeit Goods and Transnational Organised Crime*. Vienna: UNODC.

Urry, J. (2013) 'The Rich Class and Offshore Worlds'. *Discover Society*, 3. Retrieved 7/4/16, from http://discoversociety.org/wp-content/uploads/2013/11/Urry_DS3_Online.pdf.

Vagg, J. and Harris, J. (2000) 'False Profits: Why Product Counterfeiting is Increasing'. *European Journal on Criminal Policy and Research*, 8, 107–115.

van Duyne, P.C. (2003) 'The Creation of a Threat Image: Media, Policy Making and Organised Crime'. In van Duyne, P.C., Jager, M., von Lampe, K. and Newell, J.L. (eds.) *Threats and Phantoms of Organised Crime, Corruption and Terrorism: Rhetoric and Critical Perspectives*. (pp. 21–50) Nijmegen: Wolf Legal Publishers.

van Duyne, P.C. (2005) 'Crime and Commercial Activity: An Introduction to Two Half-Brothers'. In van Duyne, P.C., von Lampe, K., van Dijck, M. and Newell, J. (eds.) *The Organised Crime Economy: Managing Crime Markets in Europe*. (pp. 1–18) Nijmegen: Wolf Legal Publishers.

van Hellemont, E. (2012) 'Gangland Online: Performing the Real Imaginary World of Gangstas and Ghettos in Brussels'. *European Journal of Crime, Criminal Law and Criminal Justice*, 20, 165–180.

Vance, K., Howe, W. and Dellavalle, R.P. (2009) 'Social Internet Sites as a Source of Public Health'. *Dermatologic Clinics*, 27(2), 133–136.

Vardakou, C., Pistos C.H. and Spiliopoulou. (2011) 'Drugs for Youth Via Internet and the Example of Mephedrone'. Toxicology Letters, 201 (3), 191–195.

von Lampe, K. (2005) 'Making the Second Step Before the First: Assessing Organised Crime – The Case of Germany'. Crime, Law and Social Change, 42(4 and 5), 227–259.

von Lampe, K. (2016) Organised Crime. Los Angeles, CA: Sage.

Wagner, W.J. (no date) Cross-Border Trade in Pharmaceuticals: Free Trade or Illegal Trade. Ottawa, ON: Gowlings.

Waldron, J. (2013) Seven Arrested Over Illicit Medicines Postal Smuggling Scheme. Retrieved 30/11/13, from http://www.chemistanddruggist.co.uk/news-content/-/article_display_list/16053734/seven-arrested-over-illicit-medicines-postal-smuggling-scheme.

Walker, T. (2014) 'FedEx Facing Drug-Trafficking Charges over Illicit Pharmaceuticals'. The Independent, July 20. Retrieved 30/11/13, from http://www.independent.co.uk/news/business/news/fedex-facing-drugtrafficking-charges-over-illicit-pharmaceuticals-9616936.html

Wall, D. (2001). Crime and the Internet. London, Routledge.

Wall, D. (2007). Cybercrime: The Transformation of Crime in the Information Age. Cambridge: Polity.

Wall, D. and Large, J. (2010) 'Jailhouse Frocks: Locating the Public Interest in Policing Counterfeit Luxury Fashion Goods'. British Journal of Criminology, 50(6), 1094–1116.

Walsh, C. (2011) 'Drugs, the Internet and Change'. Journal of Psychoactive Drugs, 43 (1), 55–63.

Ward, K.J. (1999) 'The Cyber-Ethnographic (Re)construction of Two Feminist Online Communities'. Sociological Research Online, 4 (1). Retrieved 07/04/16, from http://www.socresonline.org.uk/4/1/ward.html.

Webber, C. and Yip M. (2013) 'Drifting On and Off-line: Humanising the Cybercriminal'. In Winlow, S. and Atkinson, R. (eds.) New Directions in Crime and Deviancy. (pp. 191–205). London: Routledge.

Wei, H. (2013) 'Magnetic Attraction'. China Daily, 4(135), 1, 6.

Weiss, A.M. (2006) 'Buying Prescription Drugs on the Internet: Promises and Pitfalls'. Cleveland Clinic Journal of Medicine, 73, 282–288.

Wertheimer, A.I. and Wang, P.G. (eds.) (2012) Counterfeit Medicines Volume I: Policy, Economics and Countermeasures, Hertfordshire: ILM.

Whitehead, P. and Antonopoulos, G.A. (2014) 'Payment by Results' in the Criminal Justice System in England and Wales'. The Justice Report (Canadian Criminal Justice Association), 29(1), 29–31.

WHO. (2012) Substandard/Spurious/Falsely Labelled/Falsified/Counterfeit Medical Products: Report of the Working Group of Member States. Geneva: WHO.

Winlow S. and Hall S. (2013) Rethinking Social Exclusion: The End of the Social?. London: Sage.

Wittel, A. (2000) 'Ethnography on the Move: From Field to Net to Internet'. *Qualitative Social Research,* 1(1), Retrieved 8/8/13, from http://nbn-resolving.de/urn:nbn:de:0114-fqs0001213.

Woerndl, M., Papagiannidis, S., Bourlakis, M. and Li, F. (2008) 'Internet-Induced Marketing Techniques: Critical Factors in Viral Marketing Campaigns'. *International journal of business science and applied management,* 3(1), 33–45.

Wohl, S. (1984) *The Medical Industrial Complex.* New York: Harmony Books.

World Economic Forum. (2015) State of the Illicit Economy. Retrieved 8/4/16, from http://www.csrinternational.org/govresearch/state-of-the-illicit-economy.

World Finance. (2012) 'Trade in Illegal Medicine Hits Pharmaceutical Sector'. *World Finance,* April 20.

Wright, O. (2012) 'GPs Face Pressure to Prescribe Cheaper Drugs'. *i from the Independent,* December 31, p. 5.

Yar, M. (2005) 'A Deadly Faith in Fakes: Trademark Theft and the Global Trade in Counterfeit Automotive Components'. *The Internet Journal of Criminology.* Retrieved 07/04/16, from http://www.internetjournalofcriminology.com/yar%20-%20a%20deadly%20faith%20in%20fakes.pdf.

Yar, M. (2006) *Cybercrime and Society.* London: Sage.

Yar, M. (2008) 'The *Other* Global Drugs Crisis: Assessing the Scope, Impacts and Drivers of the Global Trade in Dangerous Counterfeit Pharmaceuticals', *International Journal of Social Inquiry,* 1(1), 151–166.

Yar, M. (2012) 'Sociological and Criminological Theories in the Information Era'. In Stol, W. and Leukfeldt, R. (eds.), *Cyber-safety.* Utrecht: Eleven international publishing.

Yar, M. (2013) *Cybercrime and Society.* 2nd edition. London: Sage.

Yingqun, C. (2013) 'The Long Distance Kiss that put Flowers on the Net'. *China Daily,* February 8–14, p. 20.

INDEX

A

abuse, 76
abused, 69
Active Pharmaceutical Ingredient
    (APIs), 23, 88
Adderall, 67
addiction, 70–1
ADHD, 55–6
adhocracy, 81
adulteration, 20–1
advertising, 3, 6, 7, 31, 39–41, 44–5,
    50, 53, 55, 64, 78, 91, 98,
    103–4, 116
aesthetic, 115
affiliate, 37–40, 42, 43, 45, 53, 94,
    95, 106. *See also* subaffiliate
affordability, 23, 34, 49, 56, 76, 88
Africa, 27, 81, 82, 87, 89. *See also*
    Sub-Saharan Africa
age, 13, 57, 74, 76
alcohol, 67, 70
algorithm, 5, 32
Alibaba, 40–1
alienation, 22
Amazon, 40

amphetamine, 67–8
anaesthesia, 66
anarcho-capitalism, 41
anchor site, 106
Angola, 82, 89
anonymity, 5, 8–10, 31, 37, 41, 42,
    52, 59, 73, 106, 109
anorexia, 64
antibiotics, 28, 75
anticounterfeiting, 82
antidepressants, 28, 70
anxiety, 59
appetite suppressants, 28, 59, 63–5
assets, 93, 99, 115
AstraZeneca, 109
authenticity, 9, 54
autonomous consumer, 58–9

B

Bangladesh, 83, 87–8
banking, 23, 44, 97, 100, 103, 115
Barclaycard, 100
beauty, 41, 63, 77
Belgium, 101

© The Author(s) 2016
A. Hall, G.A. Antonopoulos, *Fake Meds Online*,
DOI 10.1057/978-1-137-57088-8

benzodiazepine, 28, 70, 75
biopharma, 110
bipolar, 58, 86
Bitcoin, 41–2
BitTorrent, 33
blockbuster drug, 36
body, 29, 60, 77, 84
bodybuilding, 7, 52, 64–5, 74, 77, 99, 106
borderlessness, 22–3
borders, 22, 25, 89, 90, 95, 108, 115. *See also* borderlessness
Brazil, 83
BRIC countries, 83, 88
Britain, 17n1, 20, 74
brokers, 54, 94, 106
buying, 5–8, 22, 48, 50, 55–7, 59, 61, 64–6, 68–70, 72, 75, 76, 92, 95, 103, 104, 106, 110, 115

C
Canada, 34
cancer, 26–8, 86, 96
capitalism, 52, 59, 83, 90, 108, 117. *See also* capitalist; latecapitalist
capitalist, 83, 117–18
channels, 16, 34, 80, 83, 85, 87–91, 94, 104, 112, 115
China, 22, 25, 40, 41, 49, 81–3, 86–90, 94, 98, 99, 101, 104, 105, 109–11, 117
clandestine, 41, 88, 89, 92–3
class, 29, 100
coating, 91, 92
cocaine, 36, 68, 75, 81–3
Colombia, 82, 88
commodification, 62
communicative capitalism, 52, 59
competition, 50, 64, 84–6, 94, 105, 109, 110
concealment, 9, 34, 44
conduits, 83, 109

conspiracy, 95, 100, 101
consumer, 2, 6, 8–10, 22, 28, 31, 35, 39, 48–54, 56–65, 68, 70, 71, 73, 74, 78, 81, 85, 114, 115. *See also* customer; user
consumerism, 49, 78
consumption, 2, 4, 25, 39, 40, 48–54, 56, 57, 62, 68–71, 73–6, 78, 87, 114–16
containerisation, 89–90
convenience, 30–1, 57, 62, 63, 65
copyright, 15, 71, 111. *See also* patent; trademark
corporeal, 3
corruption, 81
cosmetic, 28, 63, 77, 96, 115. *See also* aesthetic
costcounterfeit, 21. *See also* fake; falsification
Craigslist, 41, 98
cryptomarket, 41
culture, 2, 6, 10, 27–8, 39, 40, 47, 48, 57, 59–60, 62–3, 76, 114–17
currencies, 41–2, 43–4
customercybercrime, 23, 108. *See also* cybersecurity
cybersecurity, 37

D
darknet, 6–7, 41–2, 44–5, 49–50
dealer, 41, 53, 68, 76–7, 106–7
deception, 72
decryption, 42
deep web, 41, 44–5, 49
definitional issues, 4, 16–17, 24–5
deindustrialisation, 50
delivery, 12, 30, 35, 53, 55–6, 63, 70–1
demand, 2, 3, 6, 8, 21, 22, 24, 27, 28, 30, 47, 57, 62–5, 67–9, 71, 77, 78, 101
demographics, 9

dependency, drug, 70–1
depressants, 69
depression, 58, 59
deregulation, 21, 50, 83–4, 115–16
desire, 57–8, 60, 62, 69, 73–5, 78, 95, 115
deviance, 2, 22–3, 47–8
diabetes, 27, 28
diagnosis, 63
diaspora, 82
diet, 60, 64–5
direct-to-consumer advertising, 31. *See also* eDTCA
disembeddedness, 51–2
disembodied, 34
disorder, 59, 68–70, 86
dispersal, 116
distribution, 2, 10, 16, 22, 29, 30, 35, 36, 49, 53, 56, 78, 80, 81, 83, 85–93, 95, 97, 100, 106–8, 112, 114, 115
distrust, 48
diversification, 110
DIY healthcare, 61
doctor, 33–4, 51, 60–1, 64, 69, 72, 75, 76
domains, 42
dosage, 58, 65, 68, 93
drug diversion, 65, 76–7, 114–15
drugtaking, 50, 66, 70
Dubai, 87–8, 90

E
e-commerce, 23, 24, 31–3, 40–1, 51–2, 89, 95, 96, 103, 107–10, 112, 116
Ebay, 40–1, 96
ecstasy, 67–8
eDTCA, 31
email, 7, 35–8, 44, 50, 53, 55–6, 64, 98, 100, 103
embarrassment, 64

embeddedness, 52, 80 *See also* disembeddedness
Emirates, 90
encryption, 41, 42, 49 *See also* decryption
enforcement, 4, 5, 9, 11–13, 26, 29, 30, 114. *See also* law enforcement
England, 10–11, 69–70, 97, 99
enhancement, 76
enjoyment, 107
enteric coating, 92
entrepreneurialism,
epilepsy, 86
erectile dysfunction (ED), 9, 16, 25, 28, 35, 37, 39, 63–4, 77, 95, 96, 98–101
estrangement, 52
ethics, 8
ethnography, 5, 8–10, 35, 53, 61, 68, 73, 75, 77, 107
EU, 4, 5, 15, 17n2, 26, 30, 72, 83–7, 89, 100, 101
euphoria, 66, 67
Europe, 2, 4, 11, 20–1, 27, 81, 82, 84, 87, 89, 90, 100
exercise, 60, 64–5
experimentation, 66, 76
exports, 83

F
Facebook, 39, 41, 52–5, 76, 96, 106
factories, 22, 27, 88, 89, 91, 107–8
fake, 4, 7, 10, 15, 16, 23, 28, 30, 39, 40, 55, 58, 64, 71, 73, 75, 77, 85, 86, 93, 105
Fakecare, 3–5, 28
falsification, 15–17, 20–4, 44, 111, 114
FBI, 41
FedEx, 95
fertility, 28, 77, 114–15
finance, 4, 22. *See also* financialisation

financialisation, 21
fitness, 60
flows, 4, 22–3, 49, 87–91, 104–5, 112, 115, 116
Food and Drug Administration (FDA), 12
forums, 6–8, 13, 14, 31, 39, 40, 45, 48, 50–2, 55, 56, 59, 63, 65–7, 76, 77
fraud, 21, 29
freemarket, 78, 86–7, 111–12

G

gatekeeper, 58
GBH, 37
gender, 13, 74, 77. *See also* men; women
generics, 15, 16, 88
GlavMed, 37, 105–6, 116
globalisation, 21, 77–8, 81, 89–90, 108–9, 116, 117
glocalisation, 108
GoDaddy, 32
Google, 6–7, 35, 43, 52, 70–1, 96
Greece, 86, 97
gym, 10, 11, 64–5, 99–100, 103, 106

H

habit, 7–8, 10, 39, 55–6, 68–9, 73
hair loss, 25–6, 28, 62–3, 77, 100
hallucinations, 66–7
harm, 58–9, 62, 65, 67, 68, 71, 73, 76–8, 92, 117–18
healthcare, 9, 20, 27, 28, 34, 48, 50–63, 69, 73, 78, 85, 115–18
hedonism, 66–7
HIV, 27, 28
hormones, 27
hushmail, 36–7, 55–6

I

ideology, 78, 83–4
illness, 28, 58–9, 61–3, 75
IMF, 82
imitation, 2, 12–17, 23–4, 26–8, 43–4
India, 16, 22, 25, 29, 54, 81, 83, 87–9, 99–101, 103–5, 109–11, 117
individualism, 59
Indonesia, 83, 88
infertility, 74
Information and communications technology (ICTs), 1, 3, 4, 23, 31, 51, 52, 54, 78, 102, 112
infrastructure, 24, 31–45, 95, 103, 114, 116–18
injectable, 28, 64–5
injections, 75
Instagram, 39, 96
intellectual property rights (IPR), 15, 20, 71, 72, 105, 111–12
intermediaries, 42–4, 89, 93–6, 116
internet service provider (ISP), 12, 31–2
INTERPOL, 11, 12, 28–9
interviewing, 10–11
investigation, 4–5, 10, 14, 43–4, 96, 98–9, 101, 116
investment, 2, 36, 83
IRACM, 15, 36, 37, 81–3, 87–9, 94, 104–5
Iraq, 88, 89

J

Japan, 27
jurisdictions, 27, 30, 35, 104

K

Kazakhstan, 89, 90
KPMG, 88

L

label, 51–2, 72, 107–8

laboratory, 12, 23, 93, 108

lack, 25, 27, 33, 35, 57–9, 63, 71, 73, 83

latecapitalist, 24, 80

law enforcement, 4–5, 13, 25, 26, 28–30, 32, 33, 36, 39, 42–4, 69–70, 90, 94, 104

legal highs, 67, 68

legal loopholes, 25, 30, 44, 114

legality, 3, 53, 80, 112–14

legislation, 85–6

legitimacy, 26, 34–5, 39, 41, 105, 114

LegitScript, 11, 12, 34–5

leisure, 73

liberalisation, 56, 80, 107, 115

Liberia, 81

libertarian, 41

libertine sentiments, 66

libido, 63–4

licensing, 16, 25, 29, 30. *See also* unlicensed

lifesaving drugs, 35

lifestyle drugs, 9, 27–8, 63, 114–15

lifestyles, 9, 27, 28, 35, 44, 62–5, 77, 99, 100, 102, 103, 115

local, 3, 4, 6, 10, 60, 90, 91, 106, 108, 110–12, 114, 116, 117

logistics, 22–3, 92

Luxembourg, 85–6, 101–2

luxury, 71, 99

M

manipulation, 34, 36–8

manufacturing, 15, 22, 40, 83, 88, 91, 92, 107, 109

map, 24, 90, 91

marketing, 3, 7, 10–11, 15–16, 19–20, 23–4, 31–2, 39–41, 45, 54, 63, 64, 78, 91, 95, 103–4, 112, 116

marketisation, 21, 51–2, 56–7

marketplace, 23, 33, 40–2, 50, 103

Mastercard, 12, 32

medicalisation, 50–1, 62–3

Medicines and Healthcare products Regulatory Agency (MHRA), 11, 12, 16, 25, 26, 28, 29, 39, 44, 85, 86, 93, 95–102, 104

men, 74, 77, 106

mental health, 7, 58, 59, 114–15

merchants, 32, 35, 95–7, 99–100

methodology, 4–6, 8, 114

middlemen, 94

misuse, 69–71, 76. *See also* addiction

modernisation, 48, 50

money, 22–4, 43–4, 53, 60, 61, 70, 72, 74, 75, 94, 96, 97, 99, 102

MoneyGram, 35, 74

monopoly, 84

mood, 76

motivations, 6, 49, 54–5, 58, 61, 62, 68–9, 115

multinational corporations, 109

Mumbai, 81

muscular development, 106–7

N

narco, 81–2

narcotics, 81

National Crime Agency (NCA), 11, 12, 35–7

National Health Service, UK, 33, 48, 50–2, 56–62, 73, 115

neoliberalism, 59, 83, 116

network, 7, 8, 11, 13, 23, 33, 38, 39, 41–5, 48, 50, 51, 53, 56, 62, 63, 78, 80, 83, 86, 87, 91, 92, 95, 102, 104–7, 109, 112, 114–16

normalisation, 51, 53

O

OECD, 87
offshore, 102, 103, 115
online pharmacy, 6, 24, 32, 34, 37, 55, 103
Operation Pangea, 98
opioid analgesics, 28
opportunism,
outsourcing, 22, 92, 107
over-the-counter medicines (OTCs), 16, 27
overdosing, 70

P

packaging, 15, 24, 41, 83, 85, 89, 91–3, 97, 107, 108
pain, 76
painkillers, 55
Pakistan, 25, 36, 87, 88, 104, 110
parallel trade, 11, 30, 83–7, 89, 95, 96, 101
participatory networking, 53
patent, 15, 16, 21, 27, 41, 49, 72, 109, 111
patients, 9, 10, 34, 48, 50–2, 57–62, 72, 78, 86, 115
payment, 12, 29, 32, 33, 35, 43–5, 55–7, 74, 95–100, 103
payment gateway, 32, 33, 52, 95, 96
payment processor, 32, 55, 96, 116
PayPal, 32, 35, 52, 74, 98
PayPoint, 98
Percocet, 41, 66
Pfizer, 31, 110
pharmaceutical, 2, 19–45, 49–55, 81, 114
pharmacy, 24, 32, 34, 35, 37, 38, 55, 72, 117 online pharmacy; posting, online
platforms, 7, 20, 31, 33, 40, 88
policies, 50

policing, 71, 83
polydrug user, 66–7
porous borders, 22, 89, 90, 115
ports, 83, 90
post, 8, 13, 14, 26, 32, 33, 38, 39, 53, 66, 68, 97
posting, online, 39
pregnancy, 7, 57
prescribing, 51, 61. *See also* prescription-only
prescription-only, 69
Pretty Good Privacy (PGP), 37, 42
price, 25, 27, 35, 44, 49, 53, 56, 57, 64, 69, 70, 72–7, 84–6, 88, 95, 109. *See also* cost
privacy, 8, 58, 63, 109
privatisation, 50–5, 57–9, 61, 78
production, 2, 22, 29, 30, 40, 50–2, 54, 68, 78, 80–3, 87–93, 103–5, 108–12, 116
profit, 20, 22, 25, 27, 30, 31, 36, 71, 83–5, 94, 107, 109, 118. *See also* money; profit maximisation
profit maximisation, 30, 83, 84
prosecution, 29, 36
prosumer, 51
prosumption, 39, 52, 54, 59, 64, 106. *See also* prosumer
Prozac, 28
psychiatric, 27, 28, 59
psychostimulants, 55–6
purchasing, 6, 40, 48, 57, 96, 97, 102. *See also* buying

R

recreational drug use, 65, 67, 76
registrant, 11, 43
registrar, 11, 32, 33, 42, 43, 45, 95
regulation, 29, 30, 32, 35, 49, 60, 61, 71, 72, 78, 86, 108. *See also* deregulation

reintermediation, 52
repackaging, 85, 89, 91, 92
retail, 54, 94, 103, 110, 111, 117
revenue, 96, 97, 107
risk, 4, 5, 10, 26, 27, 30, 31, 33, 36,
    41, 48, 52, 53, 55, 57–9, 60, 62,
    67, 70, 73, 75–8, 83, 85–8, 115
Ritalin, 41, 68
Russia, 25, 81, 83, 87–9, 94

S
sales, 14, 16, 21, 29, 39, 41, 42, 50, 61,
    63, 65, 71, 72, 84, 96, 97, 103
salting, 85
Sanofi, 41
Scotland, 74, 98
sedation, 66
sedatives, 28, 69, 76, 77
seizures, 11, 25, 26, 49, 82, 101
selfgovernance, 59
sellers, 15, 23, 30, 36, 39, 41, 42, 53–5,
    74, 78, 85, 106. See also dealer
sex, 7, 28, 63, 64, 93
sharing, 67, 107
shipping, 3, 23, 30, 33, 35, 90
shopping, 23, 63
SilkRoad, 41
simulated, 54
Singapore, 86, 101
sleep, 7, 67–9
smuggling, 81, 90
social networking, 6, 7, 14, 31, 39,
    48, 50, 51, 53, 54, 63, 65, 75,
    76, 96, 107
software, 33, 41
sovereignty, 50, 59
spam email, 37, 38
Special Economic Zones (SEZs), 21,
    80, 83
stakeholders, 5, 11, 12, 33, 90, 114
statistics, 5, 11, 21, 22, 25, 26, 28

stigma, 64, 114
stimulants, 28, 55, 64, 67–9
storage, 92, 93, 97, 102
students, 76, 100, 102, 103, 115
Sub-Saharan Africa, 27
subaffiliate, 38, 42, 45, 95, 106
subcultures, 39, 65
subsidiaries, 34
substandard, 14, 16, 17, 27, 85
supplements, 65, 96, 100
supply, 2, 3, 6, 8, 9, 14, 21, 23–5,
    27–30, 33, 35, 39, 45, 48, 54–6,
    59, 62, 66, 68, 70, 78, 80, 83–6,
    91, 92, 94–6, 100, 101, 103,
    104, 106, 111, 112, 115
syndicates, 81, 108
synthetic, 23, 67, 68, 78

T
technology, 2, 22, 75, 90, 116, 117
teenagers, 70, 76, 115
testosterone, 65
Thailand, 88, 97
The Balkans, 81
The Netherlands, 24, 100
tolerance, 70–1
Tor, 42
trade, 1–4, 9–12, 15–17, 19–45,
    48–50, 52–7, 61, 63, 65, 68, 71,
    78–96, 100–5, 107–11, 113–18.
    See also parallel trade
Trade-Related Aspects of Intellectual
    Property Rights (TRIPS), 15
TradeIndia, 41, 49, 54, 106
trademark, 14, 16, 84, 85
traffickers, 81
Tramadol, 55
tranquilizers, 77
transit, 24–31, 44, 80, 81, 83, 88–91,
    95, 114
transnationalism, 108

transport, 22, 81, 90, 92, 95, 105,
     109, 112, 116
Trazodone, 66
treatment, 51, 60, 63, 74, 115
trucking, 93
trust, 54, 57–9, 61, 73, 84, 102, 107
Turkey, 26, 88, 90, 97
Twitter, 39, 96

U
United Arab Emirates (UAE), 83, 87,
     89, 90
unlicensed, 14, 16, 17, 25, 64, 95, 96,
     98, 100
UNODC, 21, 82, 94
USA, 25–7, 36, 81, 90, 95, 102
user, 6–9, 13, 14, 39, 42, 51–6, 58,
     59, 62, 64–6, 70, 75, 106, 116

V
Valium, 28, 67–9, 96

Viagra, 16, 22, 27, 28, 31, 63, 64, 74,
     75, 96

W
warehouses, 93
website, 4, 6, 7, 23, 30–3, 35,
     36, 38, 39, 42, 43, 56, 58,
     64, 84, 93–6, 98–100,
     103
weight, 7, 25, 28, 63, 77
WHOIS, 43, 45
wholesale, 21, 30, 40–1, 44–5, 49, 54,
     85, 86, 92, 94, 95, 98, 101, 106,
     115
women, 7, 64, 74, 77, 115
World Health Organisation
     (WHO), 15

Z
zones, 3, 83, 88–91, 104
Zopiclone, 40–1, 54, 66, 68–70